NOT MY FATHER'S SON

NOT MY FATHER'S SON

A Family Memoir

ALAN CUMMING

CANONGATE
Edinburgh · London

Published in Great Britain in 2014 by Canongate Books Ltd,
14 High Street, Edinburgh EH1 1TE

www.canongate.tv

1

First published in the United States in 2014 by
HarperCollins Publishers, 1985 Broadway, New York, NY 10007

Photograph on p. 14 courtesy of Getty Images,
photographer: Francois Durand; photograph of map
on p. 169 courtesy of iStock, ©studiocasper; photo still
from *The Good Wife* on p. 178 courtesy of CBS Television
Studios/photo by Justin Stephens.
All other images courtesy of the author.

British Library Cataloguing-in-Publication Data
A catalogue record for this book is available on
request from the British Library

ISBN 978 1 78211 544 1

Printed and bound in Great Britain by Clays Ltd, St Ives plc

FOR MARY D, THE TWO TOMS,
AND GRANT SHAFFER

CONTENTS

Part One

THEN
AND
NOW

THEN

You need a haircut, boy!"

My father had only glanced at me across the kitchen table as he spoke but I had already seen in his eyes the coming storm.

I tried to speak but the fear that now engulfed me made it hard to swallow, and all that came out was a little gasping sound that hurt my throat even more. And I knew speaking would only make things worse, make him despise me more, make him pounce sooner. That was the worst bit, the waiting. I never knew exactly when it would come, and that, I know, was his favourite part.

As usual we had eaten our evening meal in near silence until my father had spoken. Until recently my older brother, Tom, would have been seated where I was now, helping to deflect the gaze of impending rage that was now focused entirely upon me. But Tom had a job now. He left every morning in a shirt and tie and our father hated him for it. Tom was no longer in his thrall. Tom had escaped. I hadn't been so lucky yet.

My mother tried to intervene. "I'll take him to the barber's on Saturday morning, Ali," she said.

"He'll be working on Saturday. He's not getting away with slouching off his work again. There's too much of that going on in this house, do you hear me?"

"Yes," I managed.

But now I knew it was a lost cause. It wasn't just a haircut, it was now my physical shortcomings as a labourer, my inability to perform the tasks he gave me every weekend and many evenings, tasks I was unable to perform because I was twelve, but mostly because he wanted me to fail at them so he could hit me.

You see, I understood my father. I had learned from a very young age to interpret the tone of every word he uttered, his body language, the energy he brought into a room. It has not been pleasant as an adult to realise that dealing with my father's violence was the beginning of my studies of acting.

"I can get one tomorrow at school lunchtime." My voice trailed off in that way I knew sounded too pleading, too weak, but I couldn't help it.

"Yes, do that, pet," my mum said, kindly.

I could sense the optimism in her tone and I loved her for it. But I knew it was false optimism, denial. This was going to end badly, and there was no way to prevent it.

Every night getting off the school bus, walking through the gates of the estate where we lived, past the sawmill yard where my father reigned, and towards our house was like a lottery. Would he be home yet? What mood would he be in? As soon as I entered the house and changed out of my school uniform and began my chores—bringing wood and coal in for the fire, starting the fire, setting the table, warming the plates, putting the potatoes on to boil—I felt a bit safer. You see, by then I was on his territory, under his command, I worked for him, and that seemed to calm my father, as though my utter servitude was necessary to his well-being. I still wasn't completely safe of course—I was never safe—but those chores were so ingrained in me and I felt I did them well enough that even if he did inspect them I would pass muster, so I could breathe a little easier until we sat down to eat.

My father was the head forester of Panmure Estate, a country estate near Carnoustie, on the east coast of Scotland. The estate was vast, with fifty farms and thousands of acres of woodland covering over twenty-one square miles of land. We lived on what was known as the estate "premises", the grounds of Panmure House, though by the time we lived there the big house was long gone. In 1955, as one of many such austerity measures forced upon the landed aristocracy, its treasures were dismantled and then explosives razed it to the ground. All that remained were the stables, where on chilly Saturday mornings during hunting season I'd report, banging my wellies together to keep the feeling in my toes, to work as a beater, hitting trees with a stick in a line of other country boys, scaring the birds up into the air so that drunk rich men could shoot at them.

Attached still to the stables was the building that had been the house's chapel. Now it was used for the annual estate Christmas party and occasional dances or card game evenings for the workers. We lived in Nursery House, so called because it looked out on a tree nursery where seedlings were hatched and nurtured to replace the trees that were constantly felled and sent back to the sawmill that lay up the yard behind us. My father was in charge of the whole process, from the seeds all the way to the cut lumber and everything in between, as well as the general upkeep of the grounds.

It was all very feudal and a bit *Downton Abbey,* minus the abbey and fifty years later. I answered the door to men who referred to my father as "The Maister". There were gamekeepers and big gates and sweeping drives and follies but no lord of the manor, as during the time we lived there the place was owned by, respectively, a family shipping company, a racehorse owner's charitable trust, and then a huge insurance company.

I didn't know it at the time, but I was living through the end of an era of grand Scottish estates, as now, like Panmure, they have been mostly all dismantled and sold off. Looking back on it, it was a beautiful place to grow up, but at the time all I wanted was to get as far away as possible.

I had seen my father's van parked by the tractor shed as I walked by. So he was home. But maybe he wasn't actually in the house, maybe he was talking to one of his men in the sawmill or in one of the storehouses or sheds. It was the time of day when they were coming back from the woods and cleaning their tools before going home. I couldn't see my dad, although I didn't want to be seen to be looking for him in case he spotted me and he'd know that my fear was guiding my search. That would be his opening. Maybe there would be someone in the yard who'd come to see him, a farmer or even his boss, the estate factor (or manager), who would allow me to get by him without inspection.

I turned round the corner into the driveway of our house at the bottom of the sawmill yard, and I could see there was a light on in his office. My heart sank. He was sitting at his desk in the window and he looked up when he saw me. Immediately I straightened, tried to remember all the things he'd told me were wrong about me recently. I prayed my hair was combed the way he liked it, my school bag was hanging on my shoulder at the right angle, and my shoes were shiny enough. It probably took only ten seconds before I reached the front door and was out of his sight, but in that flash a myriad of anxieties about my flaws and failures had whirred across my mind.

He was on the phone, thankfully. He didn't come out of his office even until after my mum came home from work, and I always felt a little lighter having her in the house. She finished making our tea while we chatted. Then we heard the noise of him approaching through the house towards us and we were quiet. We both knew it was not a good idea to speak until we had appraised him, and tonight apparently it was not a good idea to speak at all.

My father sat into his chair at the kitchen table and immediately my mother set down his plate of food in front of him. This is how it always happened. Any deviation, let alone any complaint about the food, could start him off. Without acknowledging her or me he lifted his cutlery and began to eat. He ate like an animal, not because he was messy or noisy, but because he *tore* at his food, with strength and stealth and efficiency. It was terrifying to watch.

My father was silent for a while after my mum spoke, and I hoped that my going to the barber's during school lunch break the next day would appease him. All I could think of was getting to the end of this meal and upstairs to my homework, or better yet far into the woods with my dog to hide. But my mouth was so dry, and there was a lump of fear stuck at the top of my chest that made it hard to swallow. I had to get some water or I was going to choke, or worse, cry. I got up from the table and moved towards the sink. I picked up a glass off the draining board and began to fill it.

"What the hell do you think you're doing?" he said, not quite shouting yet, but still too loud, as though he had been waiting to say it, eager to make the next move, and now here it was.

"Eh? Did you hear me?"

"I need to drink some water," I gasped.

"Put that glass down!" Now he was shouting.

My mother said very quietly, "Ali, leave him."

My father rose from his chair and everything went red. At the same time as he began shouting at me he grabbed me by the scruff of the neck and I was being dragged across the kitchen, through the living room, through the hallway, out through the porch and the front door and across the yard to the shed where we kept our bikes. He threw me up on top of a workbench. He was *baying* now, not just shouting. You couldn't understand what he was saying but I know it had to do with my hair and my water drinking and how fucking useless and insolent and pathetic I was, but it wasn't coherent. It was just pure violent rage, and it was directed at me.

There was a lone bare lightbulb hanging from the shed ceiling. I remember looking up at it as he scrambled in a drawer behind me. Soon my head was propelled forward by his hand, the other one wielding a rusty pair of clippers that he used on the sheep we had in the field in front of our house. They were blunt and dirty and they cut my skin, but my father shaved my head with them, holding me down like an animal.

I was hysterical now, as hysterical as he was, but I knew he enjoyed hearing me scream and it would be over quicker if I was quiet and limp. But that was so hard. I was in pain and shock and I still hadn't had a drink of water and I felt I was going to pass out with trying to catch my breath. All I could do was wait for the end. Eventually it was over. He pushed my head one way, then the other in order to inspect his work, then threw the clippers back in the drawer.

"You get your hair cut properly! Do you hear me?" he said, rage abating, coming down, spent.

"Yes," I tried not to whimper.

He whacked me across the back of my head and was gone. The shed door banged, and I was left to climb down from the bench. I made sure to clean up the mess. I gathered in my hands the clumps of my hair that had fallen to the floor and took them to the rubbish bin outside. I returned to the shed once more to make sure everything was back to normal, and then switched off that lone lightbulb and headed back into the house. I heard the sound of my dad's van heading up the sawmill yard and I stopped for a moment, filled with shock and relief that he was gone.

In the bathroom I drank some water from the tap. Bits of hair fell into the sink as I drank and I could feel droplets of blood on my neck. Finally I stood up and stared at my reflection.

I looked like a concentration camp inmate, and I wanted to die. Really, in that moment I wanted to die. My mum tried to tidy up the mess with scissors, to make it look less uneven, but there were patches that actually had no hair left at all, that couldn't be disguised. I would have to go to school looking like this. I cried all through the night. The next morning my eyes were so red and puffy they were almost closed, but I was glad because they detracted from my head. I told my teachers I had reached up to a high shelf and knocked over a jar of creosote and some had gone in my eyes. When asked about my hair, I said I had tried to cut it myself.

NOW

I have had more hairstyles than most men of my age have had
hot dinners.

It doesn't take a genius to work out that part of the reason I
have so enjoyed changing the colour, length and look of my folli-
cles over the years is something to do with reclaiming the power
my father took from me in this regard (as well as many others) as
a child. My hair has been blond several times, it has been short
and spiky, long and floppy, sleek, shaggy, and everything in between. I've even faced the clipper demons and shaved my own
head more than once.

It took a while to get to this place, though. In my late teens,
there were several occasions when I was in a hair salon and would
suddenly feel nauseated, and twice I actually vomited, not real-
ising till many years (and quite a lot of therapy) later that my
body was manifesting physically what I could not yet cope with
emotionally. I clearly had some deeply suppressed and deeply
painful coiffure memory. But after I had left home, and was free

from my father's grip, I began to make my hair a symbol of my own freedom. One time at drama school, in a particularly semiotic act of self-assertion, I actually agreed to my youthful locks being dyed purple by an overzealous hairdressing student and went back to the parental home for the weekend with my head held high and nothing, not a word, was said about it. (I did wear a purple sweater as well, in an attempt to divert all the attention, but still, it was ballsy, don't you think?!)

I suppose what I am saying is . . . I am okay. I survived my father. We all did—my mother, my brother and me—literally as well as figuratively. But as with all difficult things, it was a process. But more of that later.

THURSDAY 20TH MAY 2010

I am standing on the stage of a huge marquee that houses the Cinema Against AIDS Gala in the gardens of the Hôtel du Cap, just outside Cannes. I am looking out at a sea of rich, tanned, chatty French people, all sipping champagne and gossiping to each other and ignoring me and smoking, smoking, smoking.

I should point out that I am not alone on this stage. I am flanked by Patti Smith and Marion Cotillard, and the three of us are just standing there, and absolutely nothing is happening. Luckily, nobody in the audience is paying any of us any attention at all, and it feels like we are trapped in celebrity aspic.

Suddenly the reverie is broken by a sheepish voice that turns out to be my own, saying into the microphone, "Um, sorry about this delay, ladies and gentlemen, we're, eh, just waiting for Mary J. Blige to return to the stage so we can auction off a duet with her and Patti."

Patti Smith's head whipped round towards me so fast I actually felt a draft. Panic made her eyes seem even more otherworldly than I'd remembered when she'd passed me on her way to the stage earlier in the evening. Right now she was the spitting image of one of those girls in *The Crucible*, fresh from a hellish vision.

"What?" she spat. "What would we even sing together? No one told me about this!"

You may not know it but Patti Smith is prone to spitting. I first met her at a party in a New York City clothing store a couple of years earlier. She sang a few songs as cute young people in black milled around serving canapés and champagne to less cute older people in black. It wasn't very rock and roll, but then Patti changed all that. In between two of her songs, she spat. Not an "Oops I've got a little something stuck on my tongue" kind of spit, but a great big throat-curdling gob of a spit. A *loogie* as they say in the Americas. And she spat *on the carpet*. Several times.

No mention was made of Patti's spitting by anyone in the store, least of all me, when I was taken to meet her after the performance. As we were introduced I could see Patti sizing me up rather suspiciously with her Dickensian eyes.

"You're the mystery guy, aren't you?" she said, pupils widening in recognition.

"What?" I said, a little overwhelmed.

"You're the guy who hosts *Masterpiece* on PBS, aren't you?" she said, as though she herself were one of the TV detectives I did indeed introduce as *Masterpiece Mystery* host. I was just processing the fact that Patti Smith was an avid viewer of Miss Marple and Co. when she dealt me another body blow:

"I've always wanted that job," she muttered wistfully.

I made a pact with myself right there and then never to tell the *Masterpiece* people this information, as they would surely bump me and make Patti's wish come true.

Can you imagine Patti Smith coming out of the shadows in a black suit, spouting forth about Inspector Linley or some malfeasance on the Orient Express and ending each introduction with a resounding gob into a specially designed PBS spittoon? I can. It would be a lot more entertaining than that bloke in a suit with the funny accent they have on now.

Meanwhile, Marion had walked to the side of the stage and was shouting to anyone who would listen, "Do something! Do something!!"

I admired her Gallic sense of injustice, but I knew her cries would be in vain. These kinds of events, though seemingly glamorous and sophisticated from the outside, are often organised with the finesse of a nursery nativity play, and one whose teachers are all lapsed members of Narcotics Anonymous.

Patti and I were left centre stage, both numb. She was presumably running through the list of songs she and Mary J. Blige might both know, which *can't* have taken long.

I was thinking back to earlier in the evening. I had started the show with a song ("That's Life"—how sadly apposite it now seemed) and a monologue in which I was purporting to channel the spirit of Sharon Stone, the event's usual host and whose shoes I was filling, as it were. Alas, the crowd was underwhelmed. The only time the drone of chat slightly faltered was when I briefly made them think Sharon was watching the proceedings via a webcam from the film set that forbade her presence. "So make sure you bid high," I had warned. "Cos that bitch will cut you."

A small crowd had gathered at the side of the stage, some offering advice, others offering their services to fill the embarrassing gap. Suddenly Harvey Weinstein, the movie mogul and the man whose genius idea it had been to auction off the duet between Patti and Mary J. in the first place, came rushing in from a side door and blurted out that he had just been ripped a new one by Ms Blige. A visible and voluble tremor rippled throughout the gaggle of glitterati. Harvey does not get dressed down by anyone, ever, let alone a ferocious R & B legend who was on her way home when she heard her name being announced for a duet she also knew nothing about. Harvey had that detached air of someone who had just been mugged. I had a sudden thought that witnessing his encounter with Mary J. would have made a much better auction item than a duet between the two ladies, but I used my inside voice and kept that to myself. Harvey mopped the sweat from his brow and said that Mary had finally acquiesced and would be out in a moment, presumably when she had finished wiping his blood off her Louboutins.

As Mary, Harvey and Patti returned to the stage, smiling as though they had planned all this years before, I fled the tent and sneaked off to the hotel bar to drown my sorrows. I realised I had never actually liked Cannes. Well, I like *Cannes,* the actual town. What I'm not so keen on are those few weeks every May when the town is marauded by movie folk.

My first ever Cannes was in 1992, when my debut feature film,

Prague, premiered there. Looking back, it was all a giddy blur. The only film festival I had ever been to before then was back home in Scotland, when a film I had made in my last term of drama school, Gillies McKinnon's *Passing Glory,* had its premiere at the Edinburgh Film Festival in 1986. I remember that experience very vividly because it was the first time I had ever seen myself on the big screen and I was horrified by how my nose seemed to appear at least fifteen seconds before the rest of my face. A less confident man might have avoided the camera for life.

But I soldiered on, and here I was, not strolling up Lothian Road and popping into the Edinburgh Filmhouse, but cruising the Croisette and *monter l'escalier* of the Palais des Congrès! That week I realised for the first time that glamour actually had a *smell.* But also I was reminded that the industry I was in was show *business.*

Film festivals are really just business conventions, you see. It could be photocopiers, it could be shower curtains, Cannes just happens to be movies. And I think any business convention, even such a glamorous one as the Cannes Film Festival, can only be interesting for so long because too many people are talking too much about the *same thing:* their jobs or *product*—as not just photocopiers and shower curtains but also films are referred to nowadays. Now don't get me wrong, I love my job, I love talking about films, but if that's the only topic of conversation available for days at a time, I get a serious bout of ennui.

That night, in my beautiful room in the Hôtel du Cap that looked out onto the stunning terrace that sloped down to the twinkling Mediterranean where the little dinghies of paparazzi bobbed in the wake, I had funny dreams. I dreamed I was back onstage in the tent and Harvey was auctioning off a kiss with me starting at thirty thousand dollars, and nobody was bidding! The fact that this had actually happened to Ryan Gosling earlier that evening only further fuelled the nightmare.

"No, Harvey," I kept saying. "Be more realistic. Start at a hundred pounds!"

I also dreamed of my mum, feverishly knitting lots and lots of pairs of socks to give as Christmas presents to all the new Asian relations she was about to acquire.

Yes, I'll run that by you again. You see, the very next day, I was to fly to London to prepare for the filming of an episode of the BBC's *Who Do You Think You Are?*, a very popular programme in which celebrities have their genealogy investigated, and studious, balding men in tweed jackets with leather patches on the elbows help the celebs pore over ancient parchments wherein family secrets are hidden. But not for long of course, as a hitherto unpredictable secret is revealed, and then the celeb cries.

I had been asked at the end of the previous year if I would be interested in taking part in the show, and had immediately said yes. Then came the rather unnerving few months when the production company people went off and did some initial research to see whether or not my past was worthy of a full hourlong probe. In other words, they needed to determine whether my ancestors were interesting enough. Being an actor, I am very used to the notion of waiting for people to pass judgement on me—audiences, critics, awards juries, fashion police—all do it with such alarming regularity that it has *almost* ceased to be alarming. But this was different. This time the judgement was not about me, and yet it reflected on me.

And I wanted very dearly to do this show because it would give me the opportunity to get to the bottom of a mystery in my mum's side of the family, a mystery whose received explanation I had never fully bought and knew would be resolved by the programme once and for all. And hence the dream about my mum knitting socks for all those new family members I imagined I was going to unearth.

Well, actually, there were two family mysteries. The other one involved my dad's side, the Cumming clan of Cawdor. Yes, *that* Cawdor, "Glamis thou art, and Cawdor; and shalt be what thou art promised" and so on. Cawdor is a little village surrounded by forest and farmland in the north of Scotland, and Shakespeare had set *Macbeth* there without bothering to research the fact that the real Macbeths never set foot in the place because they died three hundred years or so before Cawdor Castle was even built. (This lack of attention to historical detail is more grist to the mill for my theory that Shakespeare, if he were alive today, would be writing for TV. But somewhere classy, though.)

My dad's family had been Cawdor Estate farmworkers for as far back as anyone could remember. Cut to the 1980s. Like many privately owned Scottish castles, Cawdor's lairds were feeling the pinch and so opened their home to the public, thus commencing a stream of postcards, sent to me by various friends who had toured the castle, of *this* portrait . . .

Do you think there might have been a dalliance belowstairs at some point? Perhaps the help gave a little extra? Hello?!

I am startled by the resemblance of this man, John Campbell, the First Lord of Cawdor (painted by Sir Joshua Reynolds in 1778 and hanging in the castle's drawing room to this day) to myself. I have a postcard of it in my study, and several friends have mistaken it for a still from some period movie I've done.

My imagination is pretty vivid and knows no bounds at the best of times, but now it went into overdrive, and I dreamt of future episodes of *Who Do You Think You Are?* revealing that I was in fact the rightful Earl of Cawdor, and then a special follow-up show detailing the difficulties of trading in my jet-setting Hollywood life for one of a Scottish laird dealing with grumpy American tourists and damp banquet halls.

Of course I knew that aside from going to Cawdor and wrenching a chunk of hair off the present earl's head for a DNA test— something which was *not* in the remit of the rather scholarly methods of *Who Do You Think You Are?*—there would be no way of proving the veracity of my potential claim to minor aristocracy. If some randy laird long ago got a chambermaid up the duff, thereby infusing the Cumming lineage with bluish blood, he would hardly be rushing to the village clerk to have it written in the annals for TV researchers to chance upon centuries later, would he?

No, the real mystery, and the one I was happy to learn that the show was going to focus on, concerned my maternal grandfather, Thomas Darling.

Although my mum, Mary, kept the surname Cumming after her divorce from my father, she is known to me, my brother Tom, and all our friends by her maiden name, Mary Darling. She isn't Mary, she is Mary Darling. This is mostly because her name so suits her. She *is* a darling.

I had spoken to her several times that week before I arrived in Cannes, as she had been getting more and more excited about the start of filming. It was her father that the show was going to discuss, after all, a man she last saw when she was eight years old, although he hadn't died until she was thirteen, five years later, in 1951.

This is what I knew: Tommy Darling was from the north of England, an area known as the Borders for its proximity to Scotland, and was orphaned at age two. He had married my granny and had four children—Mary Darling and her three younger brothers: Tommy, Don, and the now deceased Raymond. He was a decorated soldier in the Second World War. But after the war ended Tommy Darling never came home, ever. He joined the Malayan police force and died there in a shooting accident, and was buried in neighbouring Singapore.

But *why* had he never returned to his family? And what exactly were the circumstances of this "shooting accident"?

In the run-up to the beginning of filming, my mind raced about the possible outcomes of Tommy Darling's story, but also about the way a family can have so little knowledge of a relation only one generation away. When little is known and less is spoken about, it's so easy for glaring inaccuracies to be smoothed over by surmise and assumption. I realised that I had no idea who my granddad was, and neither did my mum or my brother. Mary Darling's mum, my beloved Granny, had died a few years before, but I never remembered her speaking of him. She had actually remarried after his death, and when her second husband died there was yet more baggage heaped on top of Tommy Darling's faint shadow.

If Mary Darling was excited, I was agog. I love a surprise, you see. I loved the fact that I would not be told by the production staff where I would be going on this odyssey until the day it actually began, and each day could mean a different country, a different continent even! I had been told only that the first week of the shoot would take place in Europe (pretty vague!) and that I would start in London but would need my passport at some point. I felt like a little boy again, that feeling that I would burst with the waiting and the suspense. And worse, although the show was normally shot in two consecutive weeks, because of my filming schedule the second week and conclusion of the story would not happen for another month. I didn't know how I was going to manage to contain myself for a whole four weeks! I did know, however, that in two days' time, on Saturday morning in London, I had an appointment with a doctor to get some required jabs for the second part of the shoot, and after a quick search on the Internet I'd discovered that the countries these inoculations were required for included Singapore, so hey ho, call me Sherlock, I was pretty sure I knew where I was going to end up.

THEN

Memory is so subjective. We all remember in a visceral, emotional way, and so even if we agree on the facts—what was said, what happened where and when—what we take away and store from a moment, what we *feel* about it, can vary radically.

I really wanted to show that it wasn't all bad in my family. I tried so hard to think of happy times we all had together, times when we had fun, when we laughed. In the interests of balance, I even wanted to be able to describe some instances of kindness and tenderness involving us all. But I just couldn't.

I spoke to my brother about this. He drew a blank too.

We remember happy times with our mum. Safe, quiet times. But as a whole family? Honestly there is not one memory from our childhoods that is not clouded by fear or humiliation or pain. And that's not to say that moments of happiness did not exist, it's just that cumulatively they have been erased by the dominant feelings that colour all of our childhood recollections.

I can remember us all in a Chinese restaurant in a nearby town. We hardly ever ate out together so when we did it was a memorable occasion. But there is something nagging too, about my memories of that place, something that jabs at my heart when I think of it. I know that at least once in the few times we went there as a family I must have been hit for some flaw my father perceived, must have tried to hide my tears and humiliation from other diners. We surely had some meals there that were free of his mood swings and his tongue and the back of his hand, but they don't stand out for me.

I can remember when I was very little in the living room at Panmure, at least four or five years old, playing horsey with my father. I see him balancing me on the foot of his crossed leg as he watched TV, and him bouncing me up and down to my squeals of delight. I remember being genuinely filled with joy in those moments. But as soon as a memory like that settles for too long in my mind, another, darker one forces it to slide to the side.

I see a freezing wintry afternoon in the sawmill yard. I am on the red bike I was given for Christmas and my father has decided that today is the day that I must ride it without stabilisers. To this moment, I have never once tried to ride without them. There is ice and snow on the ground and I see my father taking the stabilisers off and pushing me down the driveway, too fast. Every time he does so I panic and fall off, and soon he gets frustrated with my failure and pulls my trousers down and slaps me really hard on my bare bum. It is so cold I have no feeling in my toes, and barely in my fingers; it is sore for me to sit down on the seat, I am scared, I am crying, and yet somehow my father thinks I am going to be able to achieve what he has decided I must do. Each time I fall, despite my pleas and promises that I will practise and be able to ride without the stabilisers soon, I am bent over his knee, feel the blast of freezing air around my genitals, and then severe, painful slaps to my behind.

I don't remember how it ended. What I do remember is my mum washing me and getting me ready for bed in front of the living room fire later that night, and her gasping as she saw the ring of blue, black, and purple bruises that had appeared. My father came in to say good-bye before he went out for the night, and my mother admonished him for his handiwork.

"He's all right," he said, running a comb through his hair as he looked in the mirror.

"You've gone too far, Ali," my mum replied as he disappeared out the door.

Aside from visits to family, our holidays together were mostly to caravan parks in seaside towns in other parts of Scotland. I remember when I was about seven we went to Dunbar on the southeast coast and I got to play on the go-karts.

This is a photo of me, beaming in my shorts and crew cut, looking towards my mother and my father, who most likely took the picture. So it's not that every second of my childhood was filled with doom. But every second *was* filled with the possibility that in an instant my father's mood would plunge into irrationality, rage and ultimately violence. This very feeling, this possibility, is what darkens the part of my mind where my childhood stories live.

It's hard to explain how much that feeling of the bottom potentially falling out at any moment takes its toll. It makes you anxious, of course, and constant anxiety is impossible for the body to handle. So you develop a coping mechanism, and for us that meant shutting down.

Everything we liked or wanted or felt joy in had to be hidden or suppressed. I'm sad to say that this method works. If you don't give as much credence or value to whatever it is that you love, it hurts less when it is inevitably taken from you.

I had to pretend I had no joy. It will come as a shock to people who know me now, but being able to express joy was something it took me a long time to be confident enough to do. I've certainly made up for it since, and for this, I am proud and grateful.

Like any tyrant, my father was an expert at knowing how to hurt you most effectively and quickly. If Tom or I became too keen on any hobby or person, our father would ensure that they were removed from our lives instantly. Tom was a great football player, and played for a local boys' club. Eventually he began to receive interest from a professional team's scouts. Immediately our father banned him from attending the football club altogether. I had a friend from school who lived in a local village, an arty girl who played the harp and whose parents were doctors. My father became convinced, based upon nothing more than a look in her eyes, that she was a drug addict, and I was never allowed to see her again. Both instances, I realise now, screamed of my father's insecurities—of me mixing with educated people whom he felt he could not relate to, and of Tom succeeding in a field in which our father himself once had aspirations.

His actual violence towards us rarely lasted beyond one or two really hard whacks, the odd kick. I actually think the prolonged period of tension before landing his blows, as we were systematically inspected, chided and humiliated, had a far worse effect than the actual hits. This certainly contributed more to our need to shut down, as we all learned early that the best way to cope in that time when his ire was building and his cruelty unfurling was to give nothing away, to try and *become* nothing, the nothing he both thought of us and wanted us to remain.

But looking back from the vantage point of adulthood, I see that there was a definite sea change in my father's behaviour.

I think I was about eight or nine. Something transformed in him. He had always been prone to outbursts of rage, but now a darkness descended upon him that meant the glimmers of light between the outbursts disappeared. It was as though my father was deeply depressed, and now I think perhaps he was. He obviously did not want to be in his marriage, he seemed to be perpetually irritated by the existence of his children, and nothing ever seemed to please him. Indeed, the only signal we got that something did not displease him was his silence, his inertia.

Now began what I remember as a time of constant darkness, silence and fear. Being around him was like navigating a minefield. We could never relax. We were never safe. He began to go out every night. I remember sitting in the living room with my mum, hearing him getting ready upstairs. Eventually the door would open and his head would appear.

"That's me away!"

But he would be gone before the words had left his mouth, his eyes not even seeing us. It was like he was saying good-night to a pet, and eventually he stopped saying it altogether.

I didn't understand what had happened, but of course I assumed it must have been something I had done. I was always being told by him how much of a disappointment I was, both in my appearance—my hair, of course, but also my posture, my weight, my nose, my moles—as well as my inability to perform the simplest of tasks, though his lack of detail in explaining what he wanted me to do or the physical enormity of what was entailed guaranteed I would fail. Once he actually demanded I drive a tractor, though I had never done so before nor had any coaching on how to do so by him or anyone else. I tried to reason with him. Often he gave me tasks that were huge and would take till night-fall and beyond, but this was another level. Now he was asking me to actually endanger my life by operating heavy machinery and I became very, very scared. My father began to shout at me and I knew I had to meet his demand. I clambered up on the high seat. My feet didn't even reach the pedals. Of course I made a mess of it and the tractor lurched into a hedge and stalled. I was hit, and perhaps that was the first time I was relieved by the violence, because it meant the conclusion of an impossibly difficult and stressful experience.

One night, as he popped his head round the door and lobbed his customary "That's me away", I asked him, "Where are you going?"

My mum looked up from her knitting; my father stopped in his tracks. There was no malice in what I had asked. I was genuinely curious. But nobody ever questioned my father, and I could see I was on stony ground.

"D'you want to come with me?" my father replied, defensively.

"But where are you going?" I asked again.

"You tell me if you want to come and I'll tell you where I'm going."

I considered this for a moment. I knew my father was going *out*. He was dressed up a bit and he smelled of Old Spice and his hair was Brylcreemed. If he was going to the pub I wouldn't be allowed in and would have to spend the evening in his van, something I did not want. But I sensed that perhaps there was more to it than that, and I think my parents could tell.

My mum said nothing.

"So are you coming or not?" my father said after a few moments, knowing he had won.

"No," I replied, meekly.

I can't remember how I came to know, whether it was kids gossiping at school or something I overheard at home, but soon I understood that the change in my father's behaviour was because he was seeing another woman, and that Tom and I were a constant reminder of the life that trapped him.

Soon after, one sunny Sunday afternoon, we all went to the beach at Carnoustie. As I've said, it was rare we did anything together, let alone anything as carefree and exciting as a trip to the seaside. Summers are short in Scotland and we tend to take advantage of the slightest hint of sun, and that day was no exception. Every time the sun peeped out from behind the clouds we raced over the sand into the freezing North Sea, ducking under the waves for a few moments before rushing back up the beach again to the shelter of our striped windbreak, an essential component of any Scottish beach excursion.

My mum opened the Tupperware box of sandwiches she'd made and we tucked in. Just then, a woman and her son appeared. We knew them locally and they greeted my father very cordially, but I could see that the woman avoided my mother's eyes. They were invited to sit down and eat with us and they did so. Conversation was stilted, and I did my boyish best to smooth things along. But I knew. This woman was having an affair with my father. That's why we had taken this rare family outing to the beach. And not only did he have the audacity to arrange this encounter and walk them to their car, leaving Mum and me to finish our sandwiches in shameful silence, but when he came back he pretended that their appearance was a total coincidence. Even worse, he actually documented that sad day, that day when he stepped over the line of respect and made us complicit witnesses to his transgression, by taking this photograph.

FRIDAY 21ST MAY 2010, NOON

By next lunchtime I had left Cannes and was back in Nice airport, slurping down a Bloody Mary (a mandatory pre-flight ritual for me) and checking out the reports of the previous night's event online. I was happily shocked to read that, although not very forthcoming with their attention, the audience certainly coughed up the cash, as seven million dollars had been raised for AIDS research! Patti and Mary J. must have *nailed* it.

Mary Darling had left another message earlier that morning. She told me there had been a reporter from the *Sunday Mail* at her door. This wasn't unusual. Over the years my mum had encountered several tabloid reporters on her doorstep, trying to get a comment from her about something (or someone!) I had been rumoured to have done or said. Now she was quite an old hand at it. She said that this time the reporter was asking about my father, wanting to find out where he lived so they could ask him for a comment about something I had said in a recent inter-view for *The Times*.

My father had been estranged from his family for many years

by this point. The British press, particularly the Scottish branch, was fascinated by this estrangement from his celebrity son and had made several attempts over the decades to goad Mr Cumming senior into "having his say" about his lack of relationship with me. This was the usual pattern: a quote from an article I'd done for some other publication would be pounced and elaborated on, and then a suitably hysterical reaction quote would be sought, encouraged or fabricated.

I knew immediately which comments from the *Times* piece they would have latched on to. I had done an interview in support of *The Good Wife*, the television show I had recently joined the cast of, originally planned as a feature in the Relationships and Health supplement of the paper. During the course of a very wide-ranging and honest chat, the reporter had asked if it saddened me that I had no relationship with my father.

"Of course," I had said. "It's the saddest thing in my life." And it was. I explained a little of how my brother and I were still waiting for our father to take up our offer to continue a relationship with us.

But I went on to talk of my belief that the way things were now was preferable to the situation that had existed previously, and that my mother and my brother and I were happier now than when there had been contact with my father, and presumably he was happier too.

I'd said this many times before. It was true, but it was also my way of moving the conversation away from "Alan's pain" and into a more sanguine and healthy admittance that sometimes people do you a favour when they drop out of your life.

And when the discussion turned to health, and I was asked about family illness, I told the reporter that recently when I'd had my first physical with a new doctor he'd asked if cancer ran in my immediate family, and I realised that, as I'd had so little contact with my father as an adult, I didn't know. I actually knew nothing about him or his health. Then, out of the blue, in the spring of 2010, my father contacted my brother Tom to tell him he was battling cancer, and Tom and I suddenly discovered which strain of that disease's odds were genetically stacked against us.

As we were finishing, the reporter asked if I thought I would ever see my father again. I said I had thought about this a lot and imagined that the only way we might have any contact would be if he reached out as he was dying.

However, the in-depth interview was scrapped in favour of one of those shorter, pithier "What I've Learned" pieces, and a collection of my words was assembled randomly under topic headings that bore little relation to the context in which they were uttered.

"My life is so much better now that my father is not in it. He does have cancer, which apparently runs in the family. Maybe next time I see him he'll be really ill, or he'll be dying and I may not see him" is how the *Times* mash-up ran.

No wonder the *Sunday Mail* was sniffing about.

Every person in the public eye will have stories of media invasion and misrepresentation. As, sadly, there were no classes at drama school for dealing with these sorts of things, I, like many before me, fumbled my way through the years and finally developed my own way of coping with this part of my job (and my life), mostly by trying to be open and honest. I had tried to be guarded about parts of my personal life in the past, but realised the hard way that doing so came over as coyness and invited speculation.

In 1999 the *News of the World*, the most vicious of tabloids in both its disdain for facts and its methods of accruing them, ran a story implying that I was accusing my father of sexually abusing me as a child. This was completely false. I had done no such thing, nor had my father.

But again, a comment I'd made about the aftermath of playing

Hamlet, in an interview with the American magazine *Out* a few months prior, had been seized upon, misquoted, sensationalised, and then deemed irrefutable evidence of an accusation of sexual molestation.

Here's what I actually said:

> *After* Hamlet *I just suddenly changed my life. I was not divorced but separated, and I also confronted my dad, with my brother's help. We went and talked to my father about the things he'd done to us in our childhood.* Hamlet *was probably not totally the cause of that, but it unlocked boxes in my mind that were locked away in the attic. And they all came out and I had to deal with them. It caused a lot of pain to many people, including myself.*

The next day, the *Daily Record*, sister paper to the *Sunday Mail*, ran a story with the headline "Father of Bisexual Star Alan Hits Back" in which my father angrily denied my nonexistent accusations.

As you might imagine, all hell broke loose.

I was in New York at the time, about to attend the premiere of a film I was in—a remake of *Annie* (talk about the universe throwing you a curveball!)—when I got a call from Mary Darling, who'd just had her irate ex-husband on the phone. He was understandably furious: every single person he knew would have seen the story. It transpired that the *News of the World* had been camped outside his house, and now other publications were ringing his doorbell.

I felt sick. My father had terrorised me, Tom and Mary Darling throughout our lives, and was physically, mentally and emotionally abusive but he was no sexual molester. I was horrified. But my horror was not just about how awful it must be for my father to be falsely accused of such a terrible act, but also that his rage was, right now, directed once more at me. The same fear and anxiety I had lived with as a child suddenly reconsumed my life. I could hear it in my voice as I spoke to my mother. I could hear it in hers. I could feel it within myself.

But worst of all was the fact that my father might think I actually *had* accused him of these things. My father did not really know me. He had no way of contacting me, as we hadn't spoken in years at that point. He also had no experience of dealing with the press or understanding of their disregard for reason in pursuit of a scandal.

In New York City, Cumming junior was smiling for the cameras in an Alexander McQueen ensemble between frantic phone calls to see what could be done to calm his father, comfort his mother, take the tabloids to task, and demand an apology for this libel. Cumming senior, at home in Scotland, also did what he felt was right: he talked. To his credit he said he didn't want to carry on a conversation with his son via the pages of a national newspaper, but of course he *was* saying that in the pages of a national newspaper.

Eventually I was able to secure an apology from the *Daily Record*. My publicist had told me that there was no way I could take on the *News of the World*, which had a renowned huge legal fund purely for quashing lawsuits from the aggrieved subjects of its stories, as well as the knowledge that anyone who wanted to pursue them had to countenance an already painful story being raked through the papers all over again should they go to court.

And although the few contrite lines at the bottom of the *Daily Record*'s Letters page a few weeks later were a far cry from the screaming headlines of the original story, it was important to me for my father to know I had done all I could to right the wrong. I wanted to show him that I cared about such an intrusion to his private life, that I was doing what I could to protect him.

Of course at the same time I was reminded that my father had never shown those kindnesses towards me, and I wondered how different such an intrusion would have felt if he had known immediately that he could pick up the phone, tell me there were reporters outside his door, and hear my advice and my reassuring words.

So now, back in the lounge at Nice airport, I listened to Mary Darling's lilting Highland tones and knew what to expect. Probably a gossipy, needling piece in that Sunday's *Mail*, no big deal compared with what had come before, but able to churn up old sadness nonetheless.

"But don't you worry, pet," she said reassuringly. "I just said I couldn't help them, had no comment, and smiled and shut the door."

My flight to London was called. I took a last sip of my Bloody Mary and thought to myself, *"Tomorrow's chip paper!"* And it was true: by Monday lunchtime the *Sunday Mail* would be used for wrapping up greasy bags of chips in fish-and-chip shops all over Scotland.

But by then, the damage would have been done. So much more damage than I could ever have countenanced.

We ascended into a cloudless Mediterranean sky and, as I always tend to do when airborne, I smelled the roses. Maybe it's the fact that I hurtle through the sky in a metal-fatigued box so regularly and therefore the odds of said box careering to a watery grave must be quite scarily higher than for the average traveller that makes me count my blessings in this way. Or maybe it's the copious amounts of free booze. Whatever, it's another inexorable ritual.

But I smell the roses not just to remind myself of how lucky I am, but also to wonder how on earth it all happened. I smell the roses to try and figure out how I came to be in the garden at all.

THEN

Nobody disliked the rain more than my father. All of a sudden nature would not bend to his will, time would not mould to his form. His meticulous plans would have to be altered. Men would have to be redirected to new, hastily created tasks. The rain brought chaos to his carefully constructed realm. And on this particular day, I would become the unwilling, and as usual ill-informed, brunt of his frustration.

This day was the first time I truly believed I was going to die. I looked into my father's eyes and I could see that in the next few moments, I might leave the planet. I was used to rage, I was used to volatility and violence, but here was something that transcended all that I had encountered from him before. This was a man who had nothing to lose. The very elements were raging against him, and what was one puny little son's worth in the grand scheme of things? I felt like I was my father's sacrifice to the gods, a wide-eyed, bleating lamb that he was doing a favour in putting out of its misery.

It was during my summer holidays from secondary school. I was old enough to be working for him full time by then, but not yet fully grown enough to be sent to aid the men with their tasks. So not only was I feeble and weak and inept, I also, in this current downpour, demanded more time and planning and attention due to my inadequacies. It was always like this with the rain. I longed for it as respite from the backbreaking labour, but as soon as it came, I knew I was doomed.

We had been working outside in the nursery, separating the one- and two-year-old spruce saplings that were strong enough to be taken to the forests and planted from the runts of the litter. These, much like me, needed to be cast aside. The rain had necessitated that this work be postponed, and instead all the saplings were transported into the old tractor shed in the sawmill yard, where they could be graded and selected in a dry place. This, I was told, was to be my job. I was sent to the shed to await further instructions.

There was a single bare lightbulb hanging above me. I stood beneath it, surrounded by mounds and mounds of spruce saplings, hearing my father's voice come wafting through the gale as he ordered his men around.

Finally the shed door opened and a gust of wind and a clap of thunder heralded his entrance. In the lightbulb's dim hue, his lumbering frame cast a shadow over me and much of the piles of baby trees. I remember the smell of them, so sweet, fresh and moist.

"You go through these," he said, picking up a handful of saplings, "and you throw away the ones like this . . ."

He thrust out a hand to me, but it was full of saplings of various lengths and thicknesses. With his shadow looming over me I could barely discern the differences between any of them.

"And you put the good ones into a pile over here." He gestured to his right.

I looked up at him, blinking and windswept.

"How do I know if they're good or not?" I asked.

"Use your common fucking sense," he said from the shadows. A second later a shaft of eerie grey-blue light filled the shed, thunder vibrated beneath my feet, and he was gone.

For the next few hours I sifted through the trees like a mole, blinking and wincing in the semi-darkness. After a while the saplings began to blur into a prickly procession, spilling through my fingers. I would check myself and go back through the discarded pile at my feet and wonder if I had been too harsh in my judgement. The pile of rejected saplings seemed to be bigger than the successful ones, and I questioned if my criteria were too harsh. Then pragmatism would win over and I'd tell myself I needed to be ruthless, that this pile had to be shifted and it never would be by prevaricating or becoming sentimental.

Of course my father had not given me much to go on to make my choices. He was usually vague and generalised in his instructions, but incredibly specific when it came time to inspect my work. But today was different. Perhaps because he was so preoccupied with the challenges the weather had created for him and his workers, he had doled out fewer instructions than usual about how I was to proceed. For instance he gave no indication of what ratio of plants should be kept to those that should be rejected. He gave no clues as to the criteria I should use in filtering them, aside from that shadowy fist he had thrust in my face. I was standing in a freezing, damp, dark room surrounded by thousands of baby trees. I began to panic.

I did what I could. When my hands began to get numb I pushed them between my thighs and held my legs close together to bring some life back into them. At times I felt I was on a roll, but then the panic would set in. I would glance down at a mound of discarded trees and realise I had been too hasty in my judgement. They seemed too healthy, too thick, too tall. But I couldn't save them all, could I?

Every moment of doubt was compounded by the knowledge that I was wasting precious time and before long my father would return. And of course, he did.

I heard him saying good-night to some of his men, and my heart sank. With none of them around, he would have less motivation to rein in his fury. After a while I heard his footsteps and the door opened slowly. He stood for a second, silhouetted, dripping and silent, as though this was how he wanted me to remember him.

I stood up from the bundles of plants and tried to ease back into the shadows.

My father bent down to one of the piles I had made and without looking up at me asked, "What are these?"

"Rejects," I said, questioningly.

He sifted through them for a moment and then, without warning, he backhanded me across the face. I flew through the air and landed in a heap against the stone wall of the shed. I was breathless and dizzy, the wind knocked out of me. I knew I had to get away. I began to run for the door, but my father grabbed on to my collar with one hand and smashed my mouth with his other. I fell to the ground and instinct told me to stay there. I could tell he had only started.

"What the fuck do you call this?" he railed.

The storm raged outside and it was as though my father was determined to belittle nature with his own wrath.

I could only whimper, "I'm sorry." I didn't know what I was

sorry for. I didn't know what he wanted, I didn't know what I was supposed to do. All I knew was that a line had been crossed. My face was throbbing and the back of my head hurt from where it had landed against the stone wall.

I was on my knees before him and he was throwing plants on me, kicking me and screaming at me. I had apparently rejected perfectly good saplings and at the same time retained puny ones that should have been destroyed. There was no rhyme or reason. All I could do was hope it would be over soon, but he continued to spew insult and bile and his body at me while the crash of the storm covered the sound.

Suddenly there were spikes in my eye and I realised he had kicked me into a pile of saplings, and then I felt the dull thud of his boot against my tailbone and my mouth was full of them too. I wanted to stay there, facedown, curled into a foetal position, and let him finish me off. But the overpowering survival instinct took over, and before he could strike again I turned round and fell to my knees before him, sobbing and beseeching.

"I'm sorry! I'm sorry! I didn't know! You didn't tell me!"

I felt pathetic but it stopped him in his tracks.

"I didn't do it on purpose. I wanted to get it right, but you didn't tell me. I'm sorry. I won't do it again. I'm so sorry. Please!"

I was done. Nobody was coming to save me, and nobody cared.

My body began to shudder and heave with such black grief that it surprised even me.

The sound of the shed door banging shut opened my eyes. He was gone. After a while I stopped crying. There were little trees stuck to my hair and in my mouth. My face was throbbing from his blows and my bum hurt from his boot.

In the eaves of the attic room of the shed was a wooden hutch my father had built to house a pair of doves we had once been given years before. For some reason I wanted to go up there. I climbed the stairs and dropped to my knees, staring plaintively into the dark recesses of the empty coop. Time passed. The storm finally subsided. The numbness in my cheek ebbed into a swelling. Darkness fell. Still I sat in a heap in front of the empty birdcage, tears flowing.

I had thought earlier I might die. Now, once again, I wanted to.

FRIDAY 21ST MAY 2010, 5 P.M.

I n no time at all I was in my London flat, having a laugh with friends.

I was to be based there for the first week of shooting of *Who Do You Think You Are?* aside from the mystery trips I would be taking elsewhere. My old friends Sue and Dom were there to greet me and I looked forward to catching up and having a laugh about the insanity of the night before in Cannes, each anecdote more sweet in its telling because it was now just that, an anecdote, and not real life.

I could relate the palpable drama after the auctioneer told Jennifer Lopez her dress made her look like an ostrich, but not have to see it, or *feel* it. There would be no anxiety that the name of the celebrity I was about to announce would not be the same as the one who walked onstage. There would be no celebrities at all, in fact. Just me and my besties.

Sue and I had met many years ago at the Donmar Warehouse theatre in London. I was there playing Hamlet, immediately followed by my turn as the Emcee in *Cabaret* that later transferred to Broadway, and we had been best friends ever since. When people ask how we met, Sue likes to tell them she washed my undies, and indeed she did, for then she was a member of that most noble of professions, the theatre dresser. She was also, and is, totally gorgeous. Quite literally, actually. Her surname had originally been Gore, but she changed it legally to Gorgeous, after years of it being her unofficial monicker. The actual document she had to sign to complete the name-changing process was hilarious, asking her to solemnly swear to renounce the name Gore and to be, from that day forth, forever Gorgeous. And she has been. When she married Dom, I and our other bestie, Andrew, were male bridesmaids, stifling our giggles as Sue walked down the aisle to Elvis singing "It's Now Or Never".

As the wine flowed and the laughter rose, I felt the feeling I most enjoyed—home. Then, Sue's phone rang.

"Hi Tom," she said. "Oh, he's here. He arrived about an hour ago." I wondered why my big brother would call Sue and not me to find out my whereabouts. Sue passed me her phone, and immediately I knew something was wrong.

"How are you doing?" Tom asked, a little shaky. Obviously he hadn't intended to speak to me.

"I'm good. How are you?" I replied, cautiously.

"When am I going to see you then?"

"Tomorrow night, remember? We're all having dinner," I said, referring to the plan for him, his wife, Sonja, a bunch of my London friends, and me to meet up in my favourite Chinese restaurant the next evening.

"I really need to talk to you, Alan."

There was silence for a moment. I tried to process what this meant.

"Well, why don't you come up a bit early tomorrow and have a drink with me at the flat before dinner?" I said eventually.

"No, I need to talk to you sooner than that." Tom was trying to hold it together, but the cracks were beginning to show.

"Tom, what's wrong?"

"I can't tell you on the phone, Alan."

"Is it your health?" My mind immediately raced to the worst possible scenarios. My brother is a rock. If he acted like this, it meant there was really something badly wrong. "Has something happened between you and Sonja?"

"No, no."

I could hear Tom, even in the midst of whatever painful thing he was dealing with, trying to reassure me. It was what he always had done for me.

"Is something wrong with Mum?" But I'd spoken to Mary Darling several times that week and had listened to a message from her just that day. There was no way she could have hidden anything bad from me.

Suddenly, I remembered what Mary Darling had said about the reporter. "Is it something to do with that *Sunday Mail* guy looking for Dad?"

"It's all come to a head, Alan," was Tom's response. "I need to talk to you tonight."

It took Tom three hours to get to me. He lives in Southampton and had to catch a train, and what with travel to and from the stations, I had to endure three whole hours of my mind racing and my heart thumping. Sue and Dom tried to distract me, but I could never wander far from the worry. What could possibly be making my brother so upset that he couldn't even utter it to me on the phone? I was a mess. My mind went to very dark places. The press being involved was a particularly disturbing element.

If I had had the ability at that moment to be rational, I would have realised that there was nothing particularly scandalous about my life that had not been revealed or touched on before now, and I might have taken solace from this added boon of having become an open book. But I was finding it hard to see solace anywhere. I started to get wheezy. I have asthma and one of the times it comes on is during moments of great stress. Sue is luckily a self-confessed hypochondriac and an expert on all homeopathic remedies, so before too long I had a mouthful of pills to distract me. But still the nagging anxiety persisted, and still Tom hadn't arrived. He kept texting: *I'm on the train . . . I'm nearly at Waterloo . . . I'm getting in a taxi.*

I kept replaying our phone conversation. Had my father died? Was it something to do with my husband, Grant? He was heading home to NYC now, could something have happened to him? But still at the root of it all was the reporter from the *Sunday Mail* and the fact that, as Tom had said, it had all come to a head. But what did that *mean*?

By the time he arrived I felt I had aged ten years. He entered the flat looking remarkably normal. No tears, no visible signs of torment. If anything he looked a little sheepish, as if he were embarrassed by all the fuss he must have known he'd caused by losing it on the phone. For a moment my heart leapt and I thought that maybe this revelation, whatever it might be, was not going to be as portentous and damaging as I'd feared. There were a few awkward moments of small talk and then he looked at me.

"Shall we go upstairs?"

THEN

When I was little, I was bullied by an older boy named David, on the school bus. David's dad was the head joiner on the estate where ours was the head forester. Tom, six years older than me and a year older than David, had graduated to secondary school by then, and we went our separate ways each morning. Tom went to Carnoustie and the swanky new secondary school, while I went to Monikie and the tiny Victorian stone primary school where there were only six people in my class. The bus I rode looked like something left over from the Second World War, and indeed it was. It was a big, hulking, dark blue military-transport type of thing, with two long benches that faced one another across a vast stretch of floor. The thing about that layout of course was that you could never look away from anyone. Everyone saw everyone else and everything that went on, all the time.

Every afternoon on the way home, and some mornings, I was kicked and pushed and slapped off the seat, my ears twisted back and forth, my books flung around and trodden on, the straps of my schoolbag held so I couldn't get away, and all the while, through my cries of pain and fear, his taunts that I had no big brother now to protect me were ringing in my (red and sore) ears. Luckily the journey back to the estate gates was a short one, and as soon as the bus stopped I leapt off and made a terrified bolt down the drive, much to the amusement of my tormentor and his little brothers.

It was all very *Lord of the Flies,* and I was Piggy.

David was a nice enough boy, and I realise now that his bullying of me that summer was just his way of establishing the new world order of the Monikie school bus. My brother had been the undisputed leader till he had ascended to secondary school, and so by terrorising me, David was not only defining himself as alpha male, but also as the new Tom Cumming. How better to show that your former leader's power is nought than by making his little brother cry?

But then I was mad as hell and I was not going to take it any more. I told Tom. Nothing much was said. Just a tearful confession after he asked me if everything was going okay at school without him. I almost forgot about it until one night we were cycling home from Cub Scouts. David and his siblings were in a gaggle ahead of us. Tom shouted out to David to wait up, and then told me to carry on home.

"What are you going to do?" I asked, suddenly alarmed.

"Just go home, Alan. I'll be there in a wee while."

I did as I was told, pedalling fast and whizzing through the estate gates and down the driveway, through the sawmill yard to our house and into the bike shed. My heart was racing; my mind a whirl of what awful torture or bloodshed might be taking place at that very moment on my behalf. My parents didn't seem to pick up on my nervousness. My mum looked up from her ironing and asked where Tom was when I entered the living room, and my dad kept his gaze on the TV. Minutes later Tom arrived, cool as a cucumber, and gave me a stony look that I knew meant we must *never* speak of this again.

Five minutes later, the doorbell rang and I raced out to answer it, my heart now in my mouth. I opened the door to find David, weeping and clutching his already bruising eye, being held up by his irate mum.

"Get your father!!" David's mum yelled.

My father ushered them in. Suddenly out of nowhere our living room was a courtroom, and I was both the smoking gun and the cause of the crime.

"Your son gave my son a black eye," David's mum shouted.

"Well, Tommy, is this true?" our father yelled, even though I could tell he was secretly proud.

"Yes, it is!" Tom said, pulling himself up and embracing his sins. "But David's been bullying Alan on the school bus for months now."

Everything stopped. David's teenage shame was now exposed for everyone to see. I felt so sorry for him, this skinny adolescent who had shoved me off my seat and thrown my books around and held me down and whacked me countless times. He had never made me feel as mortified as I knew he now felt.

Suddenly I was shaken from my sympathetic reverie by the realisation that the adults had stopped shouting, David had stopped crying. In fact the whole room had stopped and was now looking at me, waiting for *me* to bring the whole sorry mess to some sort of conclusion.

"Well, Alan," my dad said. "Is this true?"

The room fell quiet. I could feel my cheeks burning and everyone's eyes boring deep, laserlike into mine.

"No," I said meekly.

Much as I wanted to defend Tom's tribal quid pro quo, I also felt so sorry for David, snivelling away, the bruise around his eye colouring darker by the second. It was just too much to deal with, and I chose what I thought was the lesser of two evils. As soon as I'd denied he was my tormentor I'd burst into tears, and the adults mercifully realised they were putting a nine-year-old under too much duress, especially when there came no protestation of innocence from David. The Clarks went home, I was comforted, and the matter was never mentioned again. In some way there was an agreement between us all that justice had been served. An eye for an eye. Or more like a black eye for a series of bruises and stinging ears.

I told this story at my brother's wedding. (His third, incidentally. We Cumming boys love a wedding.) For me it is emblematic of our relationship: Tom always the protective big brother, me in awe of the enormity of his devotion and screwing things up.

FRIDAY 21ST MAY 2010, 8 P.M.

Almost forty years later, Tom is sitting across the table from me on the roof terrace of my flat, visibly shaking and seemingly incapable of beginning the speech that he knows is going to blow my world apart. He stammers and makes several false starts. I beg him to just say it. To just tell me. I am going mad with the waiting.

At first he apologises because he has already told Grant. Again I can't process what that means. He says he didn't know how best to tell me and so he called Grant for advice. Everything was whirring—my thoughts, Tom's voice, the skyline of Soho all around us. He finally manages to get out that our father had called him ten days ago.

"What did he say?" I whispered. I was shaking. I had started to cry. I was in hell. "Please Tom, *please* . . ."

Tom looked up at me, his blue eyes filled with tears too. He gulped, and finally he said it.

"He told me to tell you that you're not his son."

I learned something about myself that night, something I had no idea about. And about a month later, one sweaty afternoon on a terrace in southern Malaysia, I was reminded of it again: when I get really shocking news, my entire body tries to get the hell away as quickly as possible.

Before I had really processed what Tom had said I found myself propelling backwards, knocking over the bench I was sitting on and careening away from my brother. It felt as though I needed to push this incredible information back, give myself the space necessary to even contemplate contemplating it. Downstairs, Sue and Dom thought the sound they were hearing was Tom and me fighting, and that a body had just been flung to the floor.

"What do you mean?" I kept asking.

Tom was holding me now, trying to calm me down. This information was so far from left field it was not even *in* the field. To say it was the last thing I expected to hear was an understatement of an understatement.

"You're not his son," he said again.

Tom was crying too now, but he could see how overwhelmed I was, how much I needed more information, and fast.

"He called me a week ago, weeping . . . ," he began.

"Dad called you . . . Dad called you *weeping*?!" I spluttered. Nothing was making sense.

"Yes. He said he was never going to tell you, and was just going to leave you a letter in his will. But he knew you were doing the television show and so he wanted to tell you to stop you being embarrassed in public by finding out that way," he went on.

Tom was rubbing tears away with his thumb. I suddenly felt so sorry for him. He was still the big brother, my protector. And here we were once again, weeping and scared and clinging to each other. I thought our father had no power over us any more. I was wrong.

"Find out what, Tom?! Please try and tell me quickly. I'm scared. My heart is beating so fast. I think I'm going to have a heart attack."

Indeed, my heart was pounding so hard I felt the need to clutch both hands to my chest, just to make sure it stayed inside my body.

"You're in shock," Tom said. "Take deep breaths."

He continued. "He called me again this Thursday, and apologised for being so hysterical on the phone the first time. He said he's on a lot of painkillers for his cancer and he thinks he must have overdone it. But he wanted to assure me, well, to assure you, that it was all true, and he was going to leave you a letter telling you everything in his will, but he wants you to know now and he says if you ask Mum she'll deny it, but he's willing to take a DNA test . . ."

"Who is my father then?" I sobbed. "Who is he?!"

Tom said a name. It was not someone I knew, but a name I remembered as a family friend from long ago—from, in fact, the time and the place we lived when I was born. Just hearing that name made everything a bit less abstract. Its familiarity grounded me, and I began to calm down. My breathing became more regulated, my pulse slowed. This was real. It wasn't just a joke to hurt or scare me, like so many of my father's edicts from the past. It was real.

"What else did he say?"

"He said that he and Mum were at a dance at the Birnam Hotel in Dunkeld. Mum was gone for a while and this guy's wife said he was gone too, and Dad and the wife both started looking for them. They went all over the bar and the dance floor and then they went through into the hotel and they saw them, Mum and the guy, coming out of a bedroom together."

"And then what?"

"And then nine months later you were born," he added, like he was telling me a really fucked-up bedtime story.

I couldn't quite believe that my father wasn't doing this just to hurt me. One last hurrah, if you will, before he died. And the timing of it! How could he possibly think that *Who Do You Think You Are?* would focus on something so sensational and upsetting and undocumented? And then I remembered my father's experience of dealing with the media, and it made total sense. Was he actually trying to protect me for once? Of course, I also reasoned, he would also be protecting himself. His cuckolding going public would dent the ego of a man like him immeasurably.

I was not my father's son.

It wasn't supposed to have happened like this at all. Tom had discussed it with Grant, and they both felt that I should be told when I was home in New York, with Grant by my side. Tom planned to fly over in a couple of weeks once I had returned from filming in South Africa and tell me in as calm and protected an environment as possible. Poor Grant, therefore, had known this secret for the last few days we were in Cannes, keeping it to himself and never suspecting that events would dictate that Tom would need to tell me so soon.

What had happened was that the reporter from the *Sunday Mail* had found my father. Once again the tabloid press had managed to cause havoc in our family. Earlier that day, Tom had been driving home when my father called him, fuming and ranting about a reporter outside his front door. It is difficult to express the intensity of my father's rage. I am sure that even as a dying man it would be terrifying. Suddenly Tom saw a police car parked on the side of the road and so took the phone away from his ear for a moment. When he picked it up again our father was still railing, so Tom assured him he would deal with the matter and hung up. He panicked that our father's suspicions were correct and that the imminent shoot of my *Who Do You Think You Are?* had indeed prompted the news of my true lineage to somehow be leaked, and the idea that I might find out the news by seeing it splashed across the front page of a newspaper horrified him. He decided he had to tell me that night and called Sue to find out what time I was arriving.

After he'd spoken to me, he finished his journey home and then called our father back to tell him he'd set the wheels in motion and was on his way to tell me everything before I found out via the press. Of course this is when our father told him that the reporter hadn't mentioned anything about who my real father was, but had in fact merely wanted a comment about that *Times* article. Our father's fury was actually directed at me for having mentioned he had cancer, not that this massive secret had been exposed. Tom was distraught. But now it was too late, and he had no choice but to follow through.

"What about Mum?" I asked. "Did you talk to her about it?"

"Not yet," said Tom. "I wanted to let her know I was going to tell you but I didn't get a chancc."

"Don't!" I blurted. "Don't talk to her until this is all sorted out in my head."

Our family had always been one of secrets, of silence, of holding things in. The fact that my mother had never told me this, even in the decades since she and my father had divorced, was, perhaps surprisingly, not a surprise to me. She must have had her reasons, I thought, and whatever they were, I respected them, right now at least. It was incredible to think of my mother being the one who had strayed, when it was my father's infidelity that had so upset me as a child. Perhaps my mum's silence was even to protect my father—something we all seemed unremittingly conditioned to do. She was the most loyal person I knew, and if they had made a pact to stay silent all those years ago, it was no surprise that finally the one to break it would be him. Although I was shell-shocked by the news, I was also so glad my mother had had someone else in her life, some love, someone who hopefully treated her with kindness and tenderness. If I was the product of that, it couldn't be such a bad thing, I decided.

Tom told me more of what our father had said in the phone call, how he had suspected my mother of having an affair with this man and how when he had seen them come out of the hotel room that night all those years ago he merely said, "Well, there's no point in staying here any longer", grabbed her by the arm, and marched her home. It was never spoken of again.

"Well, there's no point in staying here any longer."

That was exactly the kind of thing I would expect my father to say in that situation—something gruff, uncaring. Though I had never imagined the idea of my father being in a situation where *he* would be the one discovering his spouse's infidelity.

You see, my father was a big philanderer. His disregard for his wife's feelings, and indeed anyone who knew him, by the audacity of how openly and often he paraded his infidelity was almost autistic in its terrible repetition, and it still manages to shock me. Everyone knew. Even when I was at primary school I was aware that he was having affairs. I can't remember exactly how I came to know, but I do remember the first time I recognised the pain that knowing gave me. I was eight years old, sitting on the grass of the playing field at Monikie Primary during lunch break. A little girl from my class was threading a daisy chain nearby.

"Why are you sad, Alan?" she asked me, out of the blue.

I hesitated, slightly shocked that my sadness was palpable. I realised I needed to learn how to hide my feelings better, even out-side the home. My training in the ways of the actor came early, you see.

I wasn't sure how to articulate it.

"Today is my mum and dad's wedding anniversary, and they're not celebrating it," I said finally, a dry lump in my throat.

It was true, but it wasn't the whole story of course. Somehow I understood that the whole truth was shameful and must not be spoken of. I understood that I had to collude, to protect my father, even though he didn't deserve it.

My father continued to have affairs throughout my childhood, and they were not subtle or discreet. He had no shame about pa-rading his conquests in public, sometimes even at the rare events our whole family, albeit separately, would attend. I remember a barn dance at a farm down the hill and watching my mother's face as my father arrived with another woman in tow. At school, I would hear little comments and jokes about his affairs. One of them was actually a teacher of mine. Now, decades later, it was all beginning to make sense. Was his brazen disregard for my mother's (and anyone else's) feelings about his affairs due to the fact that he felt justified because my mother had committed the original sin? And was this the reason for her stoic acceptance of his behaviour too?

It certainly explained the way he treated me. Hundreds of flash-backs of acts of violence and humiliation were being replayed in my mind. Now I saw them through a filter of knowing that my very existence was a reminder to my father of betrayal, even of his failure. But as Tom pointed out, our father was an equal op-portunity abuser, and I was not alone in my place as his target. Our father was just as harsh, irrational and violent to Tom.

I felt a bit calmer, even though there were still mental fireworks going off inside my head. I needed to make a plan. I knew that the shock waves of this news would not be confined to this evening. The repercussions of this bombshell would reverberate in my life for a long time to come.

"And there's another thing," Tom said. I looked up at him with dread. "Dad's considering talking to the *Mail*."

"What?!" I couldn't believe this could get any more awful.

"Not about you not being his son," Tom clarified.

"Well, what then?"

"He's angry that they know about him having cancer and they are telling him he should have his say about you before he dies," Tom's voice trailed off.

"Oh perfect. Well, good luck to him," I said. "If he wants to go down that road, that's his decision, but he'll regret it for the rest of his life. He has no idea what shit they'll make up."

I couldn't believe it. Any of it.

But at least, I was not my father's son.

It felt like someone had died. And I suppose in a way someone had. My father was dead, or at least the father I assumed to be mine, both literally and physically. I felt like I had created a narrative about my father over the last forty-five years, and now I was mourning its death.

I needed to give myself some time. I needed to recover. I knew I would eventually have to speak to both my parents, but I couldn't fathom that yet. The idea of contacting my *new* father was too daunting to even think about.

I also wanted to get off the roof! It was getting dark now, and cold. I was shivering, whether from the cold or pure shock, I didn't know. I knew that Sue and Dom would be worried sick. I wanted to put them out of their misery. Tom and I had been up there for ages. And I wanted to actually speak the words to another human being to make them real.

We went down and told Sue and Dom, and spent the rest of the night talking and drinking and marvelling at the insanity that can descend in an instant. Mostly we talked about memories from our childhood, horrible moments we had shared, somehow trying to tie them to what we now knew, reassessing and realigning.

Tom stayed over that night. We both bunked down in the sleeping loft at the very top of the flat. We were spent, dazed, cried and talked out. We said good-night and I switched the light off, but after a while I could feel him still awake across from me.

"You know, Alan, you're lucky," he whispered. "You're lucky you're not his son."

"I know," I said.

THEN

For a few days every June in Arbroath, a town about ten miles from our house, something magical called the Angus Show happened.

It was a traditional agricultural show, with sheep shearing and dog trials and Highland cows and tractors and tugs-of-war, but also vans full of household wares and trinkets being flogged by men who lured you to spend by shouting ever-decreasing prices through their tinny microphones. There were stalls selling all sorts of food that seemed to a country boy like me incredibly exotic. Things like corn on the cob and doughnuts. But the thing I liked most of all about the Angus Show was the humanity, the seething crowds of people that flooded the Victoria Park. I loved the feeling of being part of a crowd, of being one amongst many. It made me feel safe.

Every year as June drew near I'd see the posters for the show appearing on trees and telegraph poles all over the county. They were colourful and full of promise, and I yearned to be able to go. That was the thing, though. I never knew if I would be permitted to go. It would mean getting a lift from my dad, and as it was so difficult to predict his mood and his willingness to keep his promises, I came never to rely on him at all and eventually just stopped asking him for a lift anywhere. Occasionally a friend's parent would offer to pick me up, but we lived in such a remote place I rarely engineered it. Plus, I knew my father would see such an arrangement as a betrayal or an act of cowardice on my part. If I did, I would make sure to be dropped at the estate gates and not risk the friends coming anywhere near our house. This was a form of protection for my family, but as I got older it was more about protecting my self-esteem than shielding my father's potential behaviour. The older I became, the less concerned I became about people knowing what a monster he was. I was waiting for the day I could leave home and escape him.

And anyway, my brother and I biked mostly everywhere. Even as little boys we would cycle for miles up and down the hills and lanes of Angus. I seriously think the reason I have strong legs today is because my formative years were spent in daily intense exercise of them. We biked to the Cubs' and Scouts' meetings, to badminton at Monikie hall, several miles there and back, and then later when we were older we'd bike all the way to Carnoustie, at least a ten-mile round trip, starting the journey by freewheeling down the enormous hill called the Marches just south of the estate gates, exhilarated by the rush of the wind as we sped and the rush to be free of our father's rule for a few hours. Cycling back up at the end of the night was not quite so exhilarating. But hey, as I say, we both have calves to die for.

This particular summer I was thirteen. As usual I was working my entire summer break on the estate, *brashing*. Brashing involved taking a saw that was attached to a long pole and cutting away all the branches of a spruce tree as far up as you could reach and all the way down to the ground, thereby allowing the tree to send its energy up to the higher branches and grow taller faster, and also giving future foresters easier access when they came to cut it down and send it off to the sawmill.

Each morning at the crack of dawn I set off with a few older boys, our saws balanced precariously across the handlebars of our bikes, our packed lunches in bags slung round our shoulders. We would spend the day in some remote part of the estate, brashing away, regularly abandoning our work to race off in every direction to avoid the attacks by wasps whose nests we'd disturbed.

My father would come and inspect our work at least once a day. We would hear his van approaching and immediately we would double our efforts. Nobody wanted to get on the wrong side of him, least of all me. Often one of us would be called back down our row to inspect a sub-standard job on a tree. The walk of shame across the forest floor strewn with newly hacked branches was something I dreaded. He wouldn't hit the other boys, just humiliate them. I did my best to give him no reason to hit me in front of them, but sometimes it happened, and I would have to endure the awkward silence as I returned to my saw, trying not to cry, trying to will the sting in my ear or my face to go away.

One night I slumped into a chair in the living room, exhausted from my day in the forest, my hands blistered from the chafing of the saw shaft. We had no sofa, I realise now, only individual chairs. You'd think that would make the living room feel lonely and isolating, but actually I remember it as feeling safer because you could sit alone. That night my father did something very surprising.

"D'you want to go to the Angus Show this Saturday then?"

I don't think his eyes left the TV screen. *Crossroads* was on. Of course I knew he wasn't the least bit interested in a soap opera about a motel in the Midlands, yet he would rather look at it than me, even during this rare act of kindness.

"Yes," I said in the neutral, flat way I had learned was best when asked a question by him. This was manlier and offered less chance of being disappointed by showing emotion.

"Fine. We'll leave here at half past twelve on Saturday."

My mother was through in the kitchen doing the dishes and I knew she would have heard this exchange. Later, when my father was upstairs changing for his night out, she came through and sat down in the chair opposite me.

"Your father's going to take you to the Angus Show?" she said, picking up her knitting.

"Yes," I replied, avoiding her eyes. "But I don't have to go."

I felt torn. I really wanted to go, but I also wanted to show my mother that my loyalty lay with her, for we both knew what my going with my father would entail.

In the past, the only times my father had ever taken me anywhere of his own volition were bittersweet experiences. For even though I enjoyed these rare glimpses into a life that might have been—a seemingly loving dad taking his son swimming, or out to a café for a strawberry tart and a glass of pop—I knew that in so doing he had made me an unwilling accomplice in his affair of the moment. The time at the pool, years before, had been traumatising. She was waiting for us at the entrance. Neither my father nor she made any attempt to explain her appearance, and I knew better than to question it. It was a woman I knew. I even knew her husband. As I splashed around on my own in the shallow end I could glimpse them farther up, smiling and nuzzling, she with her back against the pool wall, my father facing her, his arms outstretched, gripping the ledge on either side of her, right under a sign with a big "NO" at the top, followed by a list of the sorts of behaviour not tolerated in this establishment, including, to my horror, "HEAVY PETTING"—exactly what my father and this woman were engaging in right at that very moment.

Even then, as a young boy, I was amazed at my father's brazenness. There would surely have been people they knew in this pool who would have seen them. They seemed to have absolutely no care that they might be compromising or embarrassing those people with their actions. I realised that my father had total disregard for anyone's feelings, let alone his wife's, or indeed his small son's, who at this very moment felt he was being dragged down into a cesspool of deceit and crime just by being near them. Afterwards my father informed me that the woman would be joining us for a cup of tea and that I could have a strawberry tart, a seasonal delicacy so delicious and so rarely experienced that my brother and I would speak of them in hushed tones. Even as I savoured it, I knew I was being bought.

But why did my father take me on these meetings, I have often wondered? He must have known my mum would ask me and I would tell her that we had not been alone, and while my mother seemed to tolerate my father's pandemic infidelity, she drew the line at her children being accessories. A huge row between them ensued as soon as we got home that day.

I was obviously being used by my father in some way, but how? Was I brought along to remind this woman that despite their obvious and public entanglement, he was still a family man with responsibilities, and that their affair would always have to remain just that? Or worse, was I there as a sort of decoy, to somehow show a softer, kinder side of my father to balance the more brutish front he presented to the world? Maybe he felt my being there made him and the woman seem more like a family and therefore less illicit to others around us?

Back home, giddy with both the rare attentions of my father and the sugar high of the soda and the strawberry tart, I came crashing down to earth when I saw my mother so angry. Soon after that, my Saturday mornings were no longer my own, as I was put to work on the estate, peeling posts in the sawmill or weeding the seedbeds in the nursery. It was backbreaking work, but I was glad to avoid such compromising situations. Even strawberry tarts had lost their lustre.

Now, several years later, I could sense a mile off that my father's willingness to take me to the Angus Show had conditions.

My mother looked up from her knitting and smiled kindly at me. "No, you go to the show, pet. I know how much you want to."

Saturday came, and at the appointed hour we set off in silence. I had my wages from the brashing burning a hole in my pocket. I hoped my father would let me have some time on my own to go and spend it.

We had to park far away from the showground, but I loved the walk, the sounds and smells wafting ever nearer us as we approached. My father walked with determination to the agricultural machinery section. There were stands with tractors and combine harvesters, and you could climb into their cabs and pretend to drive them. I didn't, of course. I was too old for that now, but I had done so as a little boy, and seeing other kids do it now made me happy and nostalgic for that time. Then, standing nonchalantly by a stall where you could collect leaflets and key chains with the tractor company logos on them, I saw her. It was not the woman I expected, yet she was not a stranger to me. We said our polite hellos, and they pretended it was a total coincidence we had bumped into each other in this seething mass. Then my father strode off and she followed. I knew better than to linger and dutifully scampered after them.

Thus began a weird dance. She and my father would be ahead of me, and suddenly they were gone. Fearing the wrath that would ensue if I became lost, I began to panic and scanned the area, leaping up and down to see over the heads for a sight of them. I wove my way through the crowds to rejoin them, marvelling at how quickly we had become separated and vowing to myself to be extra diligent from then on. Stalls that would normally have caught my eye I ignored. At one point we stopped at an army recruitment trailer, and as I glanced at the photos of burly men driving helicopters and tanks I waited for my father to start in on a story about his days in the forces. His National Service in the Royal Air Force was a source of great pride for him, even though, as I grew older and began to ask more questions, I realised he had only worked in his barracks' kitchens and had never seen any actual combat. Still, the order, the discipline, the unquestioning acquiescence to rule had obviously made a great impression on him. Of course it also crossed my mind that Tom and I were now his soldiers.

But the usual story of some fellow squaddie's ineptness never came that day. I looked up and my father was gone. She was gone. They had both disappeared into the crowds, and I knew in an instant that they had intended to do so, that they had in fact been trying to lose me for the last quarter of an hour. I had doggedly pursued them, fearful of my father's wrath, little knowing that he was trying to engineer their flight all along. My father had purposely abandoned me.

My instincts were that I should try to find them, but knowing that they had purposely tried to lose me quieted the panic that was rising from my stomach. I told myself that I had done everything I could. Surely my father would not have the audacity to punish me for this? I also started to make a plan. I looked at my options. It was light, there were many people around, and I had money. But I knew that telling anyone about what had happened, even the public "I've lost my dad" version, would not be tolerated by him. And taking a bus to Muirdrum and then walking the remaining several miles to the estate would be too much of a transgression also, so that was out of the question too. My only option—and I thought for certain the option my father both wanted and knew I would take—was to stay in the park, wander around until they returned, and take my chances. There was nothing else for me to do.

There's a thing in Scotland called "smirr" and it's miserable. It comes off the sea and it's not quite a rain but it's thicker than a mist. Well, right then, it started smirring.

Being alone in that showground turned out to be one of the most exciting times of my thirteen-year-old life. In the midst of one of my father's terrorising, psychotic mind games I was suddenly given freedom. I realised that whatever I did in the time it took for him and the woman to do whatever they had sneaked off to do was up to me. They hadn't just accidentally lost me in the crowd; they had run off, they had *abandoned* me. I then remembered his van being parked so far away, and wondered if the seclusion had also been part of his plan. I felt flushed with the feeling that for the first time ever, I held all the cards.

But soon that glow evaporated and I began to worry that they might not return, or worse, he would return alone and she would not be there to supply the buffer to my father's wrath that I was counting on. I felt lonely and yet liberated. Euphoric, and afraid.

At that time my brother Tom and his fiancée were busy creating their "bottom drawer," a collection of household items for their

life together that would be accrued throughout their engagement. Each time they bought or were given something to add to
it filled me with panic, for it meant that the day Tom would leave
me alone in our house was coming closer. And also I felt jealous,
for each pot or bedspread was a sign of a future, another life, and
a symbol of hope that I, as yet, could not imagine.

But now, alone in a showground with people positively bursting to sell me things, and with my wages just waiting to be spent,
I did something that filled my heart with joy, and surely held a
deeper symbolic meaning. I bought myself a dinner service!

I didn't mean to. I was thirteen, after all, and not likely to
be throwing any dinner parties for quite a while hence. But I
needed to feel comfort, I needed to know there was a future for
me that did not involve my father and a woman who was not my
mother running around like schoolchildren trying to hide from
me, dashing off to the back of a van carefully parked in a quiet
side street. I needed to imagine a home where I would not be
tormented, where I would be in control, where I would be the
one inviting others into my space, and I would be providing for
them. I needed to jump-start the process that my brother was
embarking on, for myself.

It took me ages to gin up the courage to bid. The stallholder
said he had a half dozen of the sets to sell off at this never-to-be-
repeated price, but I waited till the very end of his rant, when
he'd said it was his absolute lowest offer at least ten times, and
then I gingerly raised my hand. A box was almost thrown towards
me. I felt people looking at me sideways, wondering why an unac-
companied child was bidding for tableware in the rain. I walked
away from the crowds towards the animals' section where I sat on
a bale of hay and peered into the cardboard box of treasure, of
future, that I had just acquired. Beige and bland with seventies-

style flowers printed on every plate, bowl and cup, I thought they were the most sophisticated things I had ever seen. They were my ticket out. I would be eating off them in a place where there were buses and taxis and where I would never have to wait in a public place for hours, cold and damp, wondering if my father had concluded his liaison, and if or when he would come for me.

He did, of course. Both of them did. It was dark and the field was nearly empty and they actually had the audacity to pretend they had genuinely lost me. But I knew they were lying. The very fact that he did not explode when he saw me was immediate and total proof. And though it doesn't give me much pleasure to say it, he wasn't a very good actor.

NOW

U p until very recently I still had one of the saucers from that dinner service. The rest of the set had gradually been broken or given away to charity shops during my many moves through student flats in Glasgow and marital homes there and in London. But I always hung on to that one saucer because it was a talisman of my escape to adulthood from my dark years as a child, and reminded me of the actual day when I had the first inkling that I might actually get away.

Sadly the saucer did not survive my move to America, but I can still see it in my mind. It still glows in my heart.

SATURDAY 22ND MAY 2010

I woke up in the white attic and Tom was gone. I lay awake for some time, too exhausted to move.

The day was a blur. I had lunch with Elizabeth, the director of *Who Do You Think You Are?*, and the only moment I acknowledged anything was wrong came at the same time as the bill.

"I just wanted to say that I understand there's going to be surprises during the shoot, but can I just put it out there that . . ." I hesitated, not quite knowing how to convey what I meant. I just needed to give myself an out, somehow.

"I'm feeling a little delicate right now. You know, I've been travelling and I'm tired and a bit overwhelmed. If there is anything really big and completely from left field, you'll give me some sort of hint to prepare myself, won't you?"

Elizabeth looked me in the eye, a little taken aback.

"Well, of course, I can't tell you anything in advance, but I will be as respectful to you and your family's feelings as I possibly can."

I thought that was really tender and comforting, and exactly what I needed to hear. Of course the reality was a little less tender and comfortable.

Saturday night was spent with my London friends, people I have known and loved long, but see less and less frequently. I was in a daze throughout dinner, but acted like the person I wanted to be in that scenario: happy, secure, open. I pulled it off, mostly. Months later a very perceptive friend told me she had suspected that night that I was really ill. I was certainly not in my right mind.

All day my mind had been a constant rotation of memories of what had been inconsequential moments that now seemed full of portent. I mentally scanned all the childhood pictures of myself and Tom and remembered how I'd always joked about our different body types—Tom the skinny boy athlete with his washboard stomach and me the rosy-cheeked little brother with his wee belly. Now it made sense.

I swam that afternoon, the water the perfect place to soak up the whirring of my mind. As I was walking home I suddenly stopped outside Foyles bookshop just off Charing Cross Road. I was quiet for a few moments and then said aloud, "*That's* why I don't have a hairy chest!"

NOW

Recently I attended an interactive theatre piece in the Brooklyn Museum. Towards the end of the evening I was taken into a corner by a soft-spoken Japanese lady. She sat me down, took my hands in hers, and asked me, if the world were to end and I could choose one person to save, did I know who that person would be? I told her I did. Then she asked me if I thought that in the same circumstances, the person I had chosen would choose to save me. I said I knew that they would. She looked up at me with tears in her eyes.

"You are so lucky," she said. "Some people don't even know who they would save."

One of the good things about having had more than a few relationships before I met Grant is that when we did meet I knew quite a lot about myself. And so did he. We should have done, I suppose, we were both thirty-nine, after all. And so along with the euphoria and passion of our coming together was a conversation that was adult, honest and frank. We're all so conditioned to entering relationships hiding our baggage. Now he and I were laying ours out unashamedly and embracing it. It felt very good. It still does.

Grant is the kindest, funniest person I've ever met, and I've known some kind, funny people. I feel so lucky to have met him because I think we *should* be together. We just work. And we have the same eye colour. When I look into his I feel I am looking into myself.

SUNDAY 23ᴿᴰ MAY 2010

Grant woke me up on Sunday morning. He had arrived home in New York, listened to the messages I'd left him, and got straight back on a plane. I suddenly felt buoyed. I had so many things I needed to do. With Grant coming, I felt I could finally take a step.

I was more and more worried about the possibility of my father giving an interview to the *Sunday Mail*. I had no idea how many times reporters had come to his home over the years, but I had seen the few printed articles he had supplied quotes for, and there was no way anyone could interpret those as positive experiences, so why was he threatening to do this now? Now, of all times, when he had just announced his lack of connection to me, or *re*nounced his connection, more like. And then the panic began to set in. Was *that* what he was going to talk about? Was he going to spill the beans to the press before he had even spoken to me, or before I had a chance to talk to my mum? I wouldn't put it past him.

But that just didn't make sense. My father would never allow the last thing the world knew of him before he died to be that he had been cuckolded. *He!* But he was very ill, and Tom had said he had been weeping on the phone. It was all so out of character.

Tom had spoken to our dad again a couple of times in the past few days and informed him that I wanted to go ahead with the DNA test. He told me our father had begun to prevaricate and wanted to wait a few days before going ahead with any test. Why, I thought? What was *that* about?

I woke up on the Sunday and decided I needed to speak to the man myself. I knew from the start that I would eventually have to make this call. It was becoming ridiculous that Tom was forced to be the go-between between my father and me. This was about me, not Tom. And I could see the toll it was taking on my brother, every upsetting interaction being compounded by having to relay it back to me. Tom didn't deserve that pain.

I asked Tom for my father's phone number and called him. It went straight to voice mail. *Understandable,* I thought. He doesn't know my number. I wouldn't pick up a call to my home from a number I didn't recognise. I cleared my throat and wondered if I'd be able to say what I needed to say.

The machine beeped.

"Hello, this is Alan . . . Cumming. I'm calling to speak to my . . . to Alex . . . Cumming. I really need to talk to him about some things that I think he'll know about, and I would really appreciate it if he would call me back as soon as possible."

I thought I was about to hang up, but found myself saying more.

"It's urgent. It's really urgent, so please do call me as soon as you can. Thank you."

I recited my number and hung up. And the waiting began.

Tom had told me that my father was recuperating from an operation. He was clearly at home. In fact, Tom had spoken to him that morning and told him to expect my call. So as the minutes turned into hours, the fact that he was purposely not calling me back made me more and more angry. Yet again he had all the power. He couldn't stop himself, I thought. He was so used to keeping me weak, vulnerable, anxious. Though I imagined that part of his failure to speak to me was also due to some trepidation on his part. I wasn't scared of him any more, and I think that scared him.

I called again at 7 P.M. No answer.

My father's silence was stopping me from getting out of the hole he had just dug for me. I felt like I was back on the estate again, waiting for him to come and inspect me, but this time I was more angry and frustrated than anxious. I wanted it to be *over*.

I started to think of how I could deal with this situation if he never spoke to me. Grant had told me that I didn't need him to do a DNA test, as men hand down identical Y chromosomes to all their male offspring. Tom and I could do a test, and if the Y chromosomes didn't match, that would be proof enough that my father's story was true.

So we found the kits on the Internet and ordered them to arrive on a night I'd be back in England. Tom would come to my house, and we'd take the test. I felt I should wait up until my dad called, but eventually my fatigue won. I was utterly exhausted, but also slightly alarmed that I was going on camera the next morning looking so raddled. There was no make-up or hairdresser available to me for this shoot, no one who could disguise the effects of all I had learned. This was au naturel, baby, and I cursed myself for not being more demanding.

As we climbed up the steps into the sleeping loft, I told Grant that whatever happened, I needed to find out the truth for *myself.*

If my father gave me no more information than what he'd passed on through Tom, I was going to make it my mission to get to the bottom of the story, and go and talk to my real father if necessary. Once more I went to sleep, as I had done so many times as a little boy, with the full knowledge that I could never rely on my father.

I was forty-five years old. I had been waiting for a phone call from my father since I was twenty-nine, my age the last time we spoke.

I guess I should have known what to expect.

MONDAY 24TH MAY 2010

I n the morning I woke early and got ready. It felt like my first day of school. Despite everything that had happened since I arrived in London, I was actually excited about appearing on *Who Do You Think You Are?* There was nothing more I could do about the issue of my father, or my real father, at that moment. I decided to focus on diving into the TV show. The fact that my father had backed off from the ongoing investigation in my present almost gave me more breathing space to look forward and, dare I say it, enjoy the experience I was about to undergo from the past. My progeny issue was on hold, certainly until the DNA test kit arrived and was completed, and I was ready to fully commit to *Who Do You Think You Are?* And the reason I had agreed to the show in the first place: to solve the mystery of my maternal grandfather, Tommy Darling.

As I rang for the lift to take me down to the streets of Soho my phone rang. It was him.

"Hello there. This is Alex Cumming."

At first I didn't recognise his voice. There was kindness in it. And of course he didn't say, "It's your dad," so I was thrown all the more. I had started my day determined to take control of my feelings and my situation. Now I panicked. The bell of the lift pinged to signal its arrival. My phone would lose signal when I stepped in.

He went on: "I'm sorry I missed your calls yesterday, I was—"

"I can't speak to you now," came from somewhere inside me. "I have to go to work."

There was a pause.

"Well, don't worry about it. We'll get this sorted out."

Who was this person? He sounded *concerned.*

I suddenly remembered reading in one of the hundreds of e-mails sent to me with the details of my week that I would be done by 5 P.M. this afternoon.

"I'll call you back at five o'clock," I said firmly. I couldn't believe how calm and forceful I was being.

"Okay, five o'clock. I'll talk to you then, Alan."

I hung up, the lift door opened, and I stepped in. My legs buckled from under me, my stomach churned, and I burst into tears. I longed for that elevator to break down, to trap me there, to give me time to recover and regroup. Aside from "Hello" and "Take care" at my granny's funeral, those were the first words I had spoken to my father in over sixteen years.

I spent the next few hours being filmed wandering round Covent Garden watching the street entertainers. This material would be used for the beginning of my episode of *Who Do You Think You Are?* with the sonorous voice-over setting the scene for my story. It was a sunny day, and I looked like I didn't have a care in the world.

Nobody knows, I thought as I watched a sinewy topless man do a handstand walk over a line of hapless prone tourists. Nobody knows.

I was just so relieved to have a break from the constant buzz in my head that had started three days ago. Now I had new things to think about, new people to meet. I've never been one of those performers who purports to believe that acting is a welcome refuge, something to deflect or cover up things they can't or don't want to deal with in their real lives. I just *like* acting; that's why I do it. But that day I completely used acting to push away my present, to gain some respite from the chaos and, yes, the fear I knew I'd immediately drop back into when my attention was no longer diverted. It was just that today the part I was acting was myself, or this casual celebrity strolling around pretending not to notice the cameras.

We went to an apartment nearby to do an establishing interview about my reasons for doing the show and what I hoped to find out.

"I sort of pride myself on being connected to my Scottish heritage," I began. "But in more specific ways, I realise that I don't really know much about my family beyond the ones that are alive."

Every word I spoke seemed to me dripping with irony. And it got worse.

"You base who you are on your immediate lineage, and so if there are gaps in that, and mysteries in that, there are mysteries in you."

I switched the focus back on the direction the show was going to take, the investigation of Thomas Darling. "And my mum's dad is the family mystery. He's the black hole.

"There's a picture of him on my hallway wall and each time I go past him, it's a big zero. I know nothing."

It was true. Tommy Darling to me was just a face, a handsome face in an open-necked shirt with a strip of military honours just above his chest, a little black moustache. His expression was blank. I didn't yet know that this picture was taken only a few months before he died.

"He didn't come back after the war, and he never came home," I went on. "He died in a shooting accident. But at my granny's funeral someone sort of intimated to me that it wasn't an accident."

This, I think, had been the inadvertent catalyst to my taking on this whole odyssey and agreeing to do this show. At Granny's funeral, just five years prior, my main preoccupation had been to make sure my mum was doing okay. My other preoccupation, sadly, had been to keep away from my father's partner who, earlier, in an act that redefined inappropriateness, had blurted out that she needed to get my autograph for her granddaughter as she shook my hand in the crematorium receiving line mere minutes after we had sent my granny's coffin into the flames. I was literally struck dumb. Next to me I actually could feel the ire exuding from my brother's body and quickly placed a hand on his forearm to calm him. I hoped that my mother, just a couple of feet away, had not heard.

In a way, perhaps, the woman did me a favour. Because she had so appalled me, I was jolted out of the agitation I had been feeling as my father appeared, next in the line of people passing by.

"Hello," I nodded curtly and looked past him to the next mourner in line.

Later, as we raised a glass to Granny at a hotel in Inverness, I caught the woman's eye across the room and could see she had not been shamed but fully intended to pursue her goal. She made to approach me. I gave her a look that I hoped made clear my utter lack of willingness. It was the visual equivalent of "Back off, bitch!" Hell no, I was not to be trifled with, not at my granny's funeral, and not by this woman.

I talked to as many of Granny's old friends as possible. In one corner were a few older men, all of whom had known her for decades. We got chatting about old times. They wondered if I remembered Sam, her second husband. I said I didn't, though I loved the fact that she used to come and visit us when I was a little boy on the back of his motorbike. It was one of those memories that I had no true visual of, but a very vibrant manufactured one in my mind. It was *so* Granny.

"Did you know Tommy Darling?" I asked one of the men.

"Oh aye," he replied. "I knew him fine."

"He never came back after the war, did he?" I said.

The man really looked at me. Something cleared behind his rheumy eyes.

"No," he said enigmatically.

"And he died in a shooting accident?" I fished.

"Well, they called it an accident," came the reply.

"You don't think it was?" I tried not to sound too shocked.

Suddenly a hand was on my shoulder and a departing cousin took my attention. It wasn't till much later that night that I recalled the man's remark at all.

Back in Covent Garden we were wrapping up the interview.

"I sometimes feel that other parts of my life have been like an episode of *Dallas,* so I don't know why this shouldn't be too," I joked for the camera, but it was also true.

Some of the details of my family's dystopian past were much more in step with the plotlines of a histrionic television show than an everyday tale of country folk. For example, the husband of the woman who was chasing me around my grandmother's wake for an autograph had taken his own life when she told him she was leaving him for my father. Oh yes. And his son was in my father's employ at the time. And the doctor who was called to identify the body and sign the death certificate became, a few years later, my brother-in-law, when he married my ex-wife's sister. Thank you, cut to commercial break.

"I'm forty-five, you know, time's marching on. I just think you do become more curious about the past and . . . you want to know." God! Yes you do, Alan! Yes you do!

Elizabeth, the director, then steered me towards the first port of call in my quest. The next day I would be in Mary Darling's front room, asking my mother questions about who *her* father was.

I was told that we were leaving immediately for the train station. I thought we were staying that evening in London, but the early finish was in fact to facilitate travel. At 5 P.M. that afternoon I would not be sitting comfortably in the privacy of my own flat dialling my father's number, but on a train zooming north through the English countryside towards Scotland.

THEN

Train stations will forever mean Granny for me. When she came to visit us, my mum and I would go to Arbroath to collect her from the train station. I can still feel the excitement building in my tummy as we waited for her to appear amid the throngs. Finally I'd spot her, and as soon as she caught my eye her little face would burst into a grin, her suitcases would drop to her sides, and her arms would fling open to greet me as I sped down the platform towards her like a bolt of lightning.

I loved my granny. I think she was the first person to let me know it was okay to be different. The crafts I made at school that my father scoffed at and I was afraid to show him were not only praised by Granny but hung up on her wall. After she died my mum sent me a cross-stitch sampler I had made in primary school for her birthday.

I laughed when I saw it, all those years later, the wrong stitches, the size of my name dwarfing hers, but Granny had greeted it as though it were the most magical work of art.

When we went to stay with her in her little flat in Inverness she'd let Tom and me lie in bed with her, read comics, and eat sweets. Indeed, Granny not only encouraged us to bend the rules, she was usually the instigator. *She* was the one who'd first pulled us into the middle of the Grant Street pedestrian suspension bridge in Inverness and started jumping up and down to make the whole thing wobble, sending us into giggles and screams in equal measure. Of course after that, we did this every time we crossed.

When I was a little older, maybe eleven or so, and staying with her on my own for a weekend, she took me to the cinema. The only movies playing were X-rated, but that did not deter my granny. Somehow or other I was smuggled into the theatre for a David Essex double feature of *That'll Be the Day* and *Stardust*. I felt so incredibly sophisticated getting to see him in action, in an X-rated film no less!! I remember vividly a scene in which he is being pressured by his manager to write more songs for his album and he says the immortal line "I'm an artist, not a machine!" Granny and I thought this was hilarious and repeated it all weekend long, and indeed I still use it today. Talking of hilarious, that was her favourite and most-used word. Except in her Highland accent she pronounced it "hil-AH-rious", which somehow made it even more, well, hilarious.

As I got older I had to work every school holiday, and so my visits to see her in Inverness became fewer and far between. When Granny came to visit us, the atmosphere in the house changed. Her spirit infected everyone. My father was in better spirits and we felt safer when she was near. Even if she was there when I had to work all day, it still felt like a holiday knowing she would be at home when I returned from the forest, or as I sped down the sawmill yard for lunch. But gradually, my father's behaviour became more obvious to Granny, especially when he would disappear out every night even when she was staying. I could see the concern on her face as she glanced at her daughter when my dad popped into the living room for his "That's me away". I never heard Granny say a bad word about my father, but I know she was incredibly supportive of my mum leaving him. She always wished the best for everyone. I think I have inherited some of her mischief and *joie de vivre*, and I hope her compassion.

The last time I saw her was just after she'd had a heart attack and wasn't well enough to make her eldest son, Tommy's, sixtieth birthday celebrations. So we all gathered at her little assisted-living house before the party. She was very frail and looked a little overwhelmed at having so many people in her home, but she was still the same old Granny.

I had cropped blond hair at the time (maybe for a film role but maybe just because it took my fancy) and it was the cause of much scoffing by some family members.

"What's this, another weird haircut, Alan?" said one.

"Well, I like it!" Granny's frail little voice piped up from deep in the chair she was sunk into.

"And if I was young again I'd have my hair a different colour every week. I'd be a freak like Alan too!"

The day after her funeral, I had a sudden desire to go to the Grant Street suspension bridge and say my own good-bye to her. Funerals sometimes are to be endured, and as I've said, my main concern that day was looking after Mum. As Grant and I walked across, my heart sank. I was jumping up and down but it didn't feel nearly as bouncy and magical as it had all those years ago. But when we got to the middle it was completely as scary and fun as I'd remembered and we both leapt up and down like five-year-olds.

"Good-bye, Granny!" I shouted out to the sky. "I love you! Thank you!"

Grant was taking pictures and laughing with me. We stopped bouncing and had a hug. I felt really close to Granny in that moment and was so happy Grant was there to experience it. They had never met but I knew they would have loved each other. Still giddy we began to race back to the car like schoolboys in the playground. As Grant tried to pass me I put out my arm to stop him and suddenly his camera flew out of his hand, up, up into the sky. It banged against one suspension wire with a huge metallic clang, then another, before plunging into the freezing waters of the River Ness below.

We both stopped in our tracks, utterly shocked.

"That was weird," said Grant.

"That was Granny," I replied, quite certain.

I'm not religious in the slightest, but I do truly believe that people's energies can be present or invoked after they're gone. It was as if she wanted to be part of the fun on that bridge too. And losing the camera was her way of telling us to use our imaginations more, enjoy our memories but live in the moment. At least, that's what I have chosen to think. And whatever happened, I certainly had the moment of connection I'd craved with Granny.

MONDAY 24TH MAY 2010, LATE AFTERNOON

Outside the window, England slid by in a bucolic blur. I took deep breaths. I cleared my throat, laid out my pad and pen. This wasn't going to be easy. I needed to be strong. I had nothing to be ashamed of. I remembered the wise words of an American president that so connected with me I had them written in neon on the kitchen wall of my London flat: The only thing we have to fear is fear itself. I knew an awful lot about fear. I waited till five o'clock and pressed "call". He answered after a few rings. "Hullo?" His voice. Fainter than I remembered, but with the same Highland upward inflection as always.

"Hi, it's Alan."

"Uh-huh. How are you doing?" he asked.

"Well, obviously, I'm not doing so great."

Don't. Don't get riled.

"I have a lot of questions I'd like to ask you, and so I'd just like to get started."

I was being blunt on purpose, keeping him at bay, not allowing him to derail or entangle me.

"All right. I've had that reporter fellow down here again," he said, doing exactly that.

"Okay, I'll talk about that later. But do you think we could stick to the issue of me not being your son, for now?"

Don't mess with me, old man.

"Aye aye. I know you must have a lot of questions."

I looked down at my notes. I had made a list, with careful spaces for me to scribble down his answers. I needed to remember every second of this conversation.

"Are you certain? Are you absolutely certain?" I tried to sound flat and scientific.

"I'd never have brought it up if I wasn't certain, Alan," said my father. "I wrote you a letter about it, years ago. It's in my will. But when I heard you were doing this TV programme I didn't want you to find out that way, so that's why I called Tom."

The next question was difficult to ask. I was born on January 27, 1965, and I needed the maths to make sense. I needed it all to make sense, and so I said it.

"So you're certain you didn't have sex with Mum at any time during the months of April or May of 1964?"

"No, Alan, no. Sex had been sporadic with your mother for some time before that." Okay, that was definitely more than I wanted to know. A simple "no" would have sufficed, but I chose to be encouraged by his openness instead.

"It's why we had to move away from Dunkeld, Alan," my father proffered.

"Why?"

"The shame," he said. There it was. I knew it would rear its ugly head before too long.

"The shame of Mum having sex with someone else?" I asked, wondering if, like me, he'd imagined how this conversation would pan out, and if he thought we'd go this deep so soon.

"The shame of people knowing," he sidestepped slightly. "I was compromised in my work because I had dealings with him."

That made sense. We moved away from Dunkeld to the west coast of Scotland, near Fort William, when I was just under a year old, and stayed there till I was four, when we moved to Panmure Estate. And I remembered enough from growing up to understand how a small rural community like Dunkeld could be unbearable when everyone knew your dirty laundry.

This also made some sense of my father so blatantly flaunting his mistresses as we were growing up. Did he want my mother to feel that same pain, that shame, that slight on his manhood that he'd carried all through the first year of my life, pain that hurt so badly he moved his young family across a country to forge a new life away from it?

"Does my real father know?" I moved on.

"Oh yes, he knows. He must know. You see, he and his wife had a child, I think a son, shortly after you were born—"

"Wait, what?" I hadn't really thought through the new siblings issue. I mean, I suppose I presumed my real father had other children, but a half brother of my own age was something else.

"His wife was pregnant at the same time as Mum was?" I asked.

"Yes, they had a couple of other kids too, but she divorced him. And then, well . . ." His voice trailed off to nothing.

"What?" I wished he'd just tell me. Every pause felt like a booby trap. I couldn't trust him.

"Well, then he tried to shoot himself," said my father.

So yet another man had encountered the morass of my family and felt the only solution was to put a gun to his head. This did not bode well. This *was* an episode of *Dallas*.

"But he lived?" I managed to get out finally.

"Oh yes. He missed. His family took him away. He's fine now."

"Did he remarry?" I wondered. The cast of my life's new characters was mushrooming.

"He has a partner. I don't know if they ever married," he replied.

I looked down at my list of questions. We were moving through them swiftly. A little too swiftly, perhaps. Suddenly emotion reared its head for a second and I had to gulp it back down. I hesitated. "Sorry, it's just a lot to take in," I said, recovering.

And in that moment, that split second of contemplation, my father pounced.

"I can imagine," he said coolly. "I've had those reporter fellows at my door a few times saying things that were a shock to me."

Oh, I'm sorry, I thought we were discussing the fact that I've believed

for forty-five years that you were my father when you're not. I didn't know
we were back to talking about you, and how maligned you've been by the
tabloids. Sorry.

His narcissism knew no bounds.

I said, "You know, I'm really sorry you've had to deal with stuff
like that, but I think that if you knew me better, or at all, if you
even knew how to contact me, you could have called me up and
I'd have told you how to deal with them. And I could have told
you that what they were saying wasn't true."

I didn't want to get sidetracked. I still had so much more to ask.
But it was as if my father hadn't heard me.

"I've had them outside my door several times over the years,
always asking for my comment about something you've said . . . ,"
he continued.

"You know what, Dad?"

I called him "Dad" for the first time. It was a mistake. I had
purposely refrained up till now, but it just popped out. It made
me feel weak and a little boy again. "I understand. I really do.
I deal with the press every single day of my life. All I'm saying
is that the fact that I'm not in your life is not only the reason
they're there in the first place, but also why you don't know how
to deal with them."

"They ring my doorbell and ask me to comment . . ." He wasn't
listening. I had to take it up a notch.

"Listen to me! This is not what we're talking about today! But
I want you to know that I have always told the truth to the press.
Sometimes the truth hurts, and sometimes the truth is manipu-
lated and distorted by them, but I have never said anything to
them with the intention of hurting you."

I paused. There was silence on the line. I took the initiative. I
could see that I had a limited amount of time before my father

would be of no help to me. I was that little boy back on the estate again, weighing up whether there was a chance I could talk him down or if it was only a matter of time till I'd get hit. Only today he wouldn't hit me, just withhold what he knew I needed right now more than anything in the world: the truth. He had all the power, just the way he liked it.

I looked down at the next question on my list and said, "Who else knows?"

He named an old friend of my mum's who he thought had been told, though he couldn't be certain. His sister had broached the subject before she died. And of course the woman he now lived with, she of the suicide husband and the autograph-hunting granddaughter. And also my real father's wife of course. He said he had run into her from time to time over the years, and although he could tell she knew, they had never discussed it.

"Was Mum having an affair with him for a long time?" I hoped she had been—she deserved to have enjoyed loving attention, and I hoped she had it. But if my existence was due to just one brief moment of tenderness, then that was okay too.

"Well, I do remember not long before all this I was asked to start taking Tommy to football practice on Saturday afternoons." There was anger in his tone for the first time.

"And what, you think she was seeing him on those afternoons?" I prodded.

"I couldn't say for sure."

"But you think so?"

"Yes, I've a pretty good idea."

Again we went over the story of *that* night. The dance at the Birnam Hotel in Dunkeld. Mum was gone for a while when the man's wife came over and said her husband was nowhere to be seen either. They set off together through the crowded dance floor looking, and then back through the bar and into the hotel itself. As they climbed the stairs, a door opened and my mum appeared, the man behind her. They stood looking at each other for a moment, and then he grabbed my mother's wrist and said, "There's no point in staying here any longer," and yanked her away.

"And you never talked about it again. Ever?" I asked.

"Well, once, years later at Panmure, it nearly came up."

My father paused, reliving the moment, and then, as though he had never considered it in the intervening decades, said, "It was on your birthday, funnily enough."

I sat, stunned into silence.

I looked out the window. We were coming into one of those northern towns. Lancaster, was it? Or York. Yes, York probably.

"You must have known, Alan."

"What?" For a moment the train stopped, everything stopped.

"Come on! You must have known!" He was almost jovial, like we had jumped to the "We can laugh about it now" stage of this story. We had not.

I was dumbfounded.

"How could I possibly have known?"

My father cleared his throat and paused for effect.

"Did you not notice we never bonded?" he said. It was as though he was explaining the solution of a puzzle to me.

I spluttered.

Again he spoke. "Did you ever wonder why we never bonded?"

Now everything sped up. A series of nanosecond memories from years ago bombarded my vision: my father's furious and demented face, the stinging his hands left on me, the humiliation, the despair.

I wanted to scream out that yes, I had indeed wondered why we never bonded, but him not being my biological father was not the reason why. But I couldn't. I was quite literally stunned.

The train was moving, my heart was beating, my father was waiting for a response on the end of the line.

I felt I was out of my depth in dealing with this man.

And then I got it.

He was asking me to accept that his behaviour to me was justified because I was not his blood. He wanted me to condone my own physical and mental abuse.

"Of course I noticed we never bonded," I managed to say. "But I didn't know why. I thought you were just an angry, unhappy man," I added softly.

"Why didn't you divorce Mum?" I asked quickly. I felt like the lift doors had begun to close and I was grabbing my last chances before this conversation dissolved completely.

"I couldn't do that," he countered impatiently. "I had kids to bring up."

Yes, I know. I was one of them.

We'd been talking for a while and I had asked all my questions. I didn't know quite how you wound up a conversation like this, but I knew for sure that my father was not going to be the one to do it. And I was done.

"You know," I began, "when I think of your relationship, you were the one who always had the affairs, and so openly, and I always wondered why Mum didn't complain more about that. Is it because she felt she couldn't really complain because she had had the first affair, which had ended your marriage?"

There was a heavy pause. I thought I had gone too far.

"Well, I can't speak for your mother," he said finally, "but sometimes people stay together for the kids. They make sacrifices for them. And your mother and I waited till you were both out of the house before we separated."

Oh boy, here we go, the old "We stayed together for you kids" routine. So, not only was I, through my newfound half-breed status, responsible for my own abuse, but the fact that this abuse lasted for so many years was due to the kindness and self-sacrifice of my abuser?! Great.

My whole body felt on the brink of explosion or collapse or combustion. I had one last question.

"So my real father, where is he living now?" I asked.

It was as though I had pressed an ignition button. My father was suddenly years younger, and snarled with the power and fury of the man that haunted me:

"Don't you go bothering him!"

I was jolted back in my seat. I knew I had to keep calm, that the man who was shouting at me was not rational, and his default method of communication was shouting. I mustn't give him the excuse to feel I'd attacked him.

"I'm not going to bother him. But I've only discovered three days ago that he is my father, so I think I have the right to ask a few questions about him, don't you?"

Silence.

"Don't you, *Dad*?"

He ignored my question but told me a few details about where this man now lived. My father thought he ran a pub or a garage. I wondered if I'd ever meet him, or my half siblings. I wondered what they'd be like.

I told my father I was going ahead with the DNA test.

"I'm not sending a swab to America!" came the retort. He was angry now.

"Well, you don't need to." I explained how Tom and I would do the test ourselves. I would be in touch when I had the results. I could tell the wind had been blown out of his sails. Withholding his DNA was his last trump card. Now he was the one who would have to wait.

I put the phone down next to my pad and pen, then clasped my hands together and allowed my body to shake. My teeth began to chatter, my watch battered against the table's surface, my knees jerked involuntarily. Sunny England sped by. I pulled myself together and walked back the few carriages to join the BBC crew.

THEN

It was between Christmas and New Year, and everything was quiet and everything was white. We'd had an unusually large snowfall, which made me happy. The snow meant that everything calmed down. My father's attention was diverted away from the ordinary, from me, to the effects of the snow and the conditions of local roads. The estate workers were given days off until the snow cleared, and the normal schedule of jobs I had to do was postponed, aside from shovelling and bringing in logs. It was actually permissible to do a bit of *lolling*.

I loved the sound of the snow. It was calm and echoey at the same time, and the world felt a safer place being insulated by it.

My mum and I were watching TV. Suddenly the front door was thrown open and my father's voice began roaring for my mother. Mum and I both leapt up, terrified. It sounded like he was injured or being chased. She reached the living-room door before me, but I managed to catch a glimpse of my father, staggering slightly as he made for the front room, the posh one we never used except for when visitors came, or on Christmas. Behind him I saw Mr Shaw, the head gamekeeper, with whom my dad had obviously been drinking.

My father wasn't a drunk by any means. Like most Scotsmen, he liked a drink, but I rarely saw him in a state beyond what would be called "a bit merry", so seeing him like this now was quite shocking. I blamed Mr Shaw, and the snow. The former was known to like a drink a little too much, and the latter allowed a situation where boredom and close proximity to a drinks cabinet might lead to the current situation.

"We want whisky, woman!" my father roared as he sped by.

My mother closed the door, leaving me in the living room wondering what the outcome of their muffled, yet heated tones would be. A few minutes later my mother rushed back into the room and made for the kitchen.

"The cheek of the man," she said over her shoulder, and then re-emerged with a jug of water, presumably destined to be mixed with whisky in the front room.

"Coming in here and shouting at me like that."

Just then Tom arrived home. He asked me what had happened, and I told him.

"Dad's drunk."

"Drunk?" said Tom. "In the afternoon?"

"He's been at Mr Shaw's house and now they've come here because they ran out of whisky."

Suddenly the voices from the other end of the house grew louder and the front door opened and closed. I waited for the usual ensuing draft of cold air to slide through to us under the living-room door. Mr Shaw must have gone home. Now the voices of my parents rose to a crescendo and they both entered the living room, my mother enraged at the behaviour of her husband, my father bleary and blurry and bemused.

"Get upstairs, boys," he slurred.

"What makes you think you can come in about here and shout at me like that, asking for whisky like I'm your servant," I heard my mum say, strong and indignant, as the kitchen door closed on us.

"I'll come in here whatever way I want to," began my father. "This is my house."

Tom raced me up the stairs, and won as usual. The "Big Room" where we went to do our homework and to play games was freezing. We tried to occupy our time, reading and messing about, but we were both silently agitated about what was going on downstairs.

It was unusual for Mum to be so feisty. It signalled something changing in her, and her attitude towards our father, and although it made me nervous, I liked it. She had recently started working in the office of a grain mill in the local village. She was finding herself again.

Initially my father was very against her taking the job. For several years previously she had been taking night classes at Tom's secondary school to gain qualifications that would enable her to return to the workforce. This had not sat well with my father either, who constantly made attempts to sabotage or undermine her progress.

The most glaring and brutal example of this was one spring evening when my father had ordered Tom and me to accompany him out to the field below our house and help him catch one of our sheep that was about to lamb. As was usual on these sorts of occasions, our father would tell us to stand behind a hedgerow and then chase the stressed ewe towards us, screaming obscenities if we failed to grab its horns and wrestle it to the ground as it ran past us in fear of its life. He treated us basically as sheepdogs, often even whistling commands and expecting us to understand what he meant. That particular night we eventually caught the poor sheep and were just about to close the pen to give it some peace when our mother appeared at the top of the field, dressed for her night class.

"That's me away!" she called out, and swiftly turned on her heels to go back through the garden gates and into her car. I could sense my father's mood shifting, seeing her like this, and it came as no surprise when I heard him yell out to my mother's back, "Get down here! We need a hand!"

"I have my classes, Ali," she half stated, half pleaded.

"This animal is in distress. Get down here!"

It struck me that any stress was probably due to the fact that the sheep was heavily pregnant and we had just been making it run madly around the field for the past half an hour. I could tell that all it needed was to relax, lie down, and continue its labour.

Our mother arrived at the pen, navigating the mud and mounds of sheep faeces.

"I'll be late, Ali," she implored.

My father ignored her and turned towards us and the poor sheep.

"Get in here and help us hold down this beast," he said calmly and scarily. Tom and I looked at Mum and wondered what she'd do. What could she do? She put down her folders and notebooks and climbed over the gate to join us.

Our father made us hold down the sheep and commanded my mother to help it give birth. This meant she had to put her arm up its uterus and pull out the baby lamb. This is not an uncommon practice in the country. Often it came to me to do this because I had the smallest hands. But this time we all knew it wasn't necessary at all.

"You'd better get going, then," my father taunted her when she eventually stood up, her face speckled, her good blouse drenched in blood.

But Mum persevered, and when the job came up in the granary's office she somehow managed to persuade my father that it would not interfere with his household "requirements". Indeed, I offered to help even more with getting the tea ready each night, helping ensure that my father's regulated existence would not be disrupted. I could feel that this job was the start of something new and good.

"Boys! Tea's ready."

Tom and I looked at each other. We both wondered what was waiting for us downstairs. Mum sounded fine, in control even. But where was our father? We had heard no door slamming to signal he had gone out, so he must still be in the kitchen, and after the shouting match we had heard earlier, what dark mood would radiate from him now?

We entered the kitchen and both stopped in our tracks. My father was seated at his usual place, next to me, at the kitchen table, but he was leaning forward, head and arms sprawled across the table top. He was *out cold*. And my mother had set the table for our evening meal *around him*.

"Come on, it's all right, he won't wake up," said Mum, sensing my anxiety. It felt like I was going into the sleeping ogre's den. Tom laughed.

"Are we going to eat our tea with him just lying there?" he asked.

"Yes," said Mum calmly. "Your father doesn't seem to be hungry, but we all need to eat."

So we sat down, and awkwardly passed the butter and condiments over my father as we ate our food. Once, I looked up and saw that his eyes had opened and were staring right at me. Immediately panic seized me, but he merely swallowed, smacked his lips, and closed his eyes again.

After a while, I began to enjoy this Alice-in-Wonderland-like experience. We all did. In his drunkenness our father was no threat to us, and more than that, he was no impediment to the continuation of our daily routine. Sitting at that table night after night was terrifying. It would be again tomorrow, no doubt, but tonight, with my father snoring, and us passing the biscuit plate over his head, we could breathe easy.

Later, when we had washed the dishes and removed the table things from around him, my mother suggested we drive to Dundee to see the new film everyone had been talking about, *Jaws*. I couldn't believe my ears. I could count the number of times we had gone to the cinema as a family, or at least a part family, on the fingers of one hand. I ran upstairs to get changed in a state of ecstasy. Everything was changing this night. The idea that we would be going off to do something as luxurious and rare as driving all the way to Dundee in the snow to see a movie was exciting enough, but to do so as our father lay snoring in the darkness of the kitchen unaware was simply beautiful. And that my mother was so calm and sure in her actions made it all the more sweet.

Tom asked if he could cycle to Monikie to see his girlfriend instead of coming with us. Mum agreed. It seemed anything was possible tonight!

We set off in the car, and after we'd wound along the crispy moonlit country roads for a few minutes, Mum spoke up.

"Alan, what would you think about you and me and Tommy living on our own?"

I felt as if the heavens had opened and there was light and warmth and goodness pouring into the car. I felt God. It was almost too much. This afternoon everything had been normal. The snow had allowed some brief respite, but now it was as if the whole world had changed. I wanted to cry, I wanted to laugh, I wanted to leap across the seat and shower my mother with kisses. But I was paralysed. My mouth was dry and I could barely hear myself say . . .

"Away from Dad, you mean?"

I just wanted to be sure.

"Yes, away from Dad. Just you and me and Tommy living together. Would you like that?"

"Yes," I said, a tear plopping down my cheek. "I would like that."

Suddenly, the car hit a patch of ice and we were spinning madly out of control, forever it seemed. I thought we were both going to die. The God I had glimpsed moments ago turned out to be not so benevolent. He was the same old God, the one that quashed your dreams and kept you in line. He was the angry, vengeful *man* of a God and my Mum had dared to cross him.

By the time the car had stopped we were facing the way we had come, and my side of the car was leaning into a ditch. The engine was off and I could only hear our panicked breathing and my heart beating wildly in my little bony chest. After a few moments, Mum asked if I was okay and I whispered that I was. She started the engine, and we went on our way again, but quietly and meekly now, all triumph and elation gone.

The matter was never spoken of again.

Years later at drama school I learned of the Moirae, the goddesses who controlled everyone's fate, and the dangers of crossing them by trying to step away from the destined path we are given.

We called them Moira instead of Moirae, and our History of Drama teacher indulged us, hoping I suppose that humour would better aid our memories come exam time.

"Cumming," he said, one rainy Glasgow afternoon, "do you understand this concept? Do you know what it feels like to overstep your Moira?"

At once I was back in that car on that icy road, spinning to potential death just seconds from having heard the offer of freedom.

"Oh yes," I replied. "I understand."

TUESDAY 25ᵀᴴ MAY 2010

By 6 A.M. I was staring out my hotel-room window at the old Dundee docks. I was so tired, but my mind wouldn't let me sleep. In a few short hours I would see my mother.

I was worried she'd sense something was wrong. I felt as though there was a sign above my head declaring "MAN IN TROUBLE". I had so many questions that I wanted to, yet couldn't, ask, and certainly not in front of a TV crew. And after all, today's discoveries and revelations were not going to be about me, or my real father. I had to try and put everything about that to one side and appear my normal self. I had to act.

No matter what is going on in my real life, I know how to block it out when I am working. Whether I have had good news, bad news, am feeling hungover, joyful, sick, it's all part of the job description of an actor to know how to neutralise it all and become whatever the character needs to feel. Today was no different: I would become what the audience would expect—cheeky chappie Alan Cumming having tea with his mum and looking through old family photos and mementoes. It shouldn't require much of me. Yet looking out at the water as the sun began to slowly slide along its surface, I didn't know if I was up to it.

I went to the gym and hoped the endorphins would cancel out the buzzing in my head for a while. I met the crew for breakfast and pretty soon we were off, filming in the car as I drove along the coast road towards my mum's.

I talked of my mum as I drove, captured by the camera being pointed at me from the passenger seat. I spoke of how much I admire her, how she has rolled with the punches through the changes in my life, and how much she has grown as a person over the years. I also spoke of how she still has the ability to surprise me. Considering the events of the past few days, that was an understatement.

When we arrived at Mary Darling's house, Elizabeth, the director, and the soundman hurried over to put a microphone on her, and also shield her from seeing me so that our reunion on camera would be utterly spontaneous.

I could see my mum trying to peep over their shoulders to see me. She was brimming with excitement, I could tell. I bet she hadn't slept much the night before either, albeit for different reasons.

Soon, after we had hugged on her doorstep, we went into her living room and began to set up what would be the major part of the discussion: just what my mum knew about her father.

As the crew set up some lights, and Mum and Elizabeth conferred about what she was going to say and show me, I began to scour the walls and shelves of her lounge for all the pictures of my family. There we were, Tom and me as kids, in our swimming trunks in the garden at Panmure, on a jetty after a boat trip. Then later, university, weddings, holidays. My father was nowhere to be seen of course. My mother left him when I was twenty and away at drama school in Glasgow. She had worked hard to be financially independent of him, and then, just when I thought they had reached an amiable situation of leading entirely separate lives under the same roof, she called me up and announced she would be living at a different address from then on. For so many years I had longed for my parents to separate, but when I heard the news I was sideswiped, stunned and strangely upset. It was as though all the pent-up sadness of watching two people in such an unhappy union came flooding out of me. I hadn't realised just how much I wanted their relationship to work, I guess. I longed for a proper Mum and Dad with a normal relationship. And now it was clear that this would never happen.

Looking around at these images spanning my entire life, it was not difficult to believe that I had a different father. A weird calm descended upon me and I just knew.

"So, Mum, what do you remember of your father?" I asked her.

She was a little nervous and very cautious as she spoke. It made me love her even more. She spoke of how little she knew of the man, just that he had been in the military, a Cameron Highlander. He was stationed in Inverness where he met my granny.

Tommy Darling was twenty in 1937 when he married. Mary Darling was born a year later, and her three brothers followed in quick succession. But despite having a growing family, Tommy Darling's visits home grew less and less frequent. In the talks we'd had about him in the months preceding, I had asked my mother why she thought he had come back home so little and she said that it was common during the war for a soldier's leave to be cancelled or postponed. That made sense, I suppose, but surely a gap of five years was a little extreme?

I asked Mum where her father had gone after the war. "Well

he went to several places. He was in France and Burma," she replied.

"What did he do?" I asked. I didn't even know this most basic piece of information about him.

He was a biker, a courier who carried information amongst battalions on the battlefield. Mum then showed me a pewter mug that he had. It was one of the few things she owned that had belonged to Tommy Darling. According to the inscription, he'd won the cup at a services motorbike trial, in 1939.

"So he's a biker?" I joked. A picture of Tommy Darling was beginning to form in my mind, and he was certainly challenging my preconceptions.

She also had his Certificate of Service and I read it aloud.

"*An excellent type. Honest, sober . . .*" I looked up at Mum. "That's unusual for our family!"

"I beg your pardon!" she quipped right back.

Mum then very proudly showed me a medal he had received for bravery in the field. I had seen it as a child, but knew nothing about when or why Tommy Darling had been recognised in this way.

We talked about the circumstances of his death. In 1950 he had taken a job with the Malayan police force, and less than a year later he was dead. Mary Darling was thirteen, and she had not seen her father since she was eight. When I gently asked her the circumstances of his death, my mother quietly described the story as it had been shared with her. He had been cleaning a gun. There was still a bullet in the chamber. He had shot himself accidentally.

This was news to me. I had always remembered he had been shot accidentally on a shooting range, a stray bullet making him a victim of that particularly oxymoronic phrase "friendly fire". I suppose my boyish imagination must have just made that up.

The plot was definitely thickening.

As the interview wound up I smiled at her and gave her a kiss. I knew Mum had been anxious but she had done a really good job. Now, as she scampered through to the kitchen to begin serving the lunch she'd prepared for me and the crew, I took a moment to reflect on how similar our situations were right now—both of us on the brink of finding out the truth about our fathers. I had a flash of having to tell her what my father had revealed and how her face would crumble as I did so, but I put that thought away for now.

"Alan! Will you pour these people a glass of wine instead of just sitting there!" my mum admonished me. My reverie was broken and I snapped back into my role as dutiful son.

The next step in my investigation was to delve further into Tommy Darling's military life, and so just a couple of hours later I was at the National Library of Scotland, a beautiful building just off the Royal Mile in Edinburgh. I had actually filmed there the year before for a documentary I had made about the Scottish sense of humour, and had been very happy to discover via one of its ancient tomes that we Scots were the first to ever catalogue the word *fuck*! Now here I was again, with Tommy Darling's military records and documents spread out in front of me, poring over them with a military historian.

The first thing that struck me was why my grandfather had chosen to join the Cameron Highlanders and not a battalion closer to his home. I learned that the Highlanders had a great reputation for being a very loyal, closely knit group of soldiers. Thinking back to the fact that my granddad had been an orphan, I thought perhaps he was looking for a family in the military. A lump formed at the back of my throat.

Wow. This was going to be harder than I thought. Pouring my

attention into discovering the life of my grandfather as a way of temporarily avoiding my own past was not going to work, especially if everything I learned I could relate to how I was feeling and my experiences. I also began to see why perhaps my grandfather was such an absent father. His experience of family was so limited, maybe it was something he could never quite understand.

Tommy Darling was stationed in Inverness and worked as a cook in the barracks there. His military records painted the picture of a model soldier.

Indeed, the only negative in any of his records from this time was that one night he had been stopped by a military policeman and fined for riding his motorbike with insufficient light on his registration plate.

I looked at the wedding photographs of Tommy Darling and my granny, recognising my great-auntie Ina as a bridesmaid, and began to build a picture of the young, newly married cook, soon to be a father for the first time, full of hope for the future, building the family he never had.

Then, suddenly, everything changed.

In 1939 war broke out, and Tommy Darling extended his time in the army and volunteered as a dispatch rider for the Royal Army Ordnance Corps. Suddenly I remembered the initials RAOC that were on that pewter mug. I showed it to the historian, who examined it and told me that Tommy Darling had been given that mug for winning a trial, or a test of a motorcyclist's ability to travel cross-country under the kind of conditions that would exist in war. And pretty soon he would be experiencing war for real, as in 1940 the Cameron Highlanders were shipped off to France and into the front lines of the Second World War.

As I looked through photographs and accounts of the Allied

efforts, I learned exactly what a dispatch rider would actually have done in battle. I also began to see that Tommy Darling was a bit of a daredevil. In the space of a few hours I had found out that he'd left the comfort of the battalion depot kitchens (and his family) to serve his country in the most treacherous conditions imaginable—tearing through the mud of the French country-side delivering crucial messages from military HQ to the troops on the front lines. Suddenly he had gone from a man in a uni-form on my wall in New York, to a swashbuckling daredevil.

In 1940 the Germans had utterly overpowered the Allied troops and forced them into retreat, and the massive evacuation from Dunkirk in Normandy was being hastily planned. I discov-ered that the Cameron Highlanders were stationed forty miles south of Dunkirk and being used in a last-ditch effort to halt the German onslaught and enable the evacuation to proceed. Tommy Darling was riding his dispatch bike between battalion HQ in Violaine and La Bassée, where the Camerons were trying to stop a three-hundred-strong tank division from crossing the canal and reaching Dunkirk. It was during this time that he won the Military Medal that my mum had shown me. The historian showed me the citation for it in Tommy's regimental records:

*Lance Corporal Darling showed the greatest courage
and disregard for his personal safety in getting messages
through to the forward Companies.*

I wanted to know more. Tommy Darling was becoming real to me, and I felt a bond forming that was hard to describe. It was a concern for a man I had never met. But that was all there was.

Sensing my desire for more, the historian piped up, "This is a gallantry award of which you should feel very proud."

But then something else was revealed that connected with

me even more. The Military Medal Tommy Darling had been awarded was such a high honour that he had been invited to Buckingham Palace in 1941 to receive it. Sixty-eight years later, I, his grandson, had also been to Buckingham Palace to pick up a medal. I was awarded the OBE (Officer of the British Empire) in the Queen's Honours List of 2009 for *"services to film, theatre and the arts and to activism for equal rights for the gay and lesbian community"*, a tad less heroic and gallant than my grandfather's, but an honour nonetheless.

My mum, my brother and my husband all came to the palace that day with me. I remember Mary Darling bubbling with excitement and pride like a little girl in a fairy tale, a feathery fascinator perched on her head as she sat between Tom and Grant in the front row and waited for me to appear to collect my medal. How incredible that none of us had the slightest inkling that Tommy Darling had preceded us all there by nearly seven decades.

The crew went off to get some shots of the Edinburgh landscape and I went back to the hotel in Edinburgh's New Town alone. It was one of those boutique hotels formed by several townhouses being knocked together, and I was in the attic suite. As I ran my bath I flipped up the windows and took in the view stretching out to the Firth of Forth, enjoying the breeze wafting up from the coast. I was exhausted, and I looked it. It was when I had moments on my own that I worried that the toll of all this was too much to bear.

I closed my eyes and listened to the hum of traffic heading up towards Haymarket station or down to Stockbridge. I couldn't get the image of a photograph on my mother's wall out of my head. It was from when we lived in Dunkeld. The picture was of me, Mum and Tom. I'm just a baby; I'm standing, but a baby still. And Tom and I look like friends. Not siblings.

THEN

I am at peace. I am twelve years old, my jeans are around my
ankles, and I've just made a big discovery.

I am lying on my back on a grassy clearing that juts out over a
gully in the forest, the burn below tinkling its way to the North
Sea. I come here every night now after we've had our tea. This is
partly to escape the silence of my parents' house, but mostly to
avoid my father, and newly to enjoy what I have come to learn my
penis can do. What it's for, it seems.

If I turn my head towards the burn and press that ear into the
grass, I can hear the birds tweeting and maybe a distant cow or
sheep out of the other. It's a still spring night, brisk and hopeful.
I know if I lie here for too long I might fall asleep and then wake
up cold, flakes on my tummy where now I feel wet warmth. I
open my eyes.

There is a man standing looking at me. He is on the path at
the top of the hill, the one that runs along the edge of the forest
before it drops off to the gully floor. He is not near enough to

be physically threatening, but he has obviously just watched me ejaculate, and I know this man. He's one of the estate's forestry workers and he works for my dad. I see him every day as I walk up through the sawmill yard on my way to catch the school bus. When he sees that I see him he immediately pulls back onto the path out of sight and is gone. My heart is suddenly racing and my cheeks are flushed once more. I can feel something rising up inside me. I am instinctively resisting but it is fighting very hard for control of me. It is shame.

What have I done wrong? I ask myself. I know that boys do this. I know it's inevitable and natural. I just hadn't realised how good it would feel. So why do I feel anxious for doing what is right? Why should I feel bad because this man saw me? Why? Because he might tell my dad, and like so many others before it, this new happiness will be stamped on.

I lie there for a while in the dusk, then make a decision, little knowing how it will affect every facet of my life and fibre of my being for the rest of my life: I say no to shame. This man was the one in the wrong. He was the voyeur, however accidental.

But I didn't wish him ill. I would have done the same. I actually even thought my father would be glad to learn that some progress was being made in the faltering journey to my manhood. So I rejected shame.

I went to pull up my jeans but thought against it, and lay back down and looked up at the darkening sky. I closed my eyes.

WEDNESDAY 26TH MAY 2010

The next morning we were up with the sun and off to the train station. Today was to be mostly a day of travel, first to London's King Cross, and from there to Lille in France, where we would spend the night, and then I would be taken to the exact spot where Tommy Darling had earned his Military Medal.

Just as the man who was my new father was never far from my thoughts, I also couldn't keep the images of Tommy Darling from filling my mind on the long, quiet journey southwards. Here I was following his footsteps into war. I was forty-five. He had been twenty-four when he left for France, a father to two children with a third on the way. What can it have felt like to leave them behind and go off into combat, where every day, every time he got on his motorbike, there was a chance he'd never get to see them again?

We had a little layover at King's Cross and I wandered around the beautiful, newly renovated station. I began to wonder how all this new information was going to change my life, change me.

I thought back to the last time I had felt this shaken, to, in fact, the last time I had any dealings with my father, sixteen years before. Tom and I had travelled up to the estate to speak to him about our childhood. It did not go well. But the ensuing silence and absence of him from our lives because of this confrontation enabled us both to move on. We both felt a freedom from his legacy, and a clarity, that we had never before experienced.

For me, I found myself embracing the childhood I felt I had missed. My flat began to fill with games I had either played as a boy or lusted after. I discovered I loved the colour yellow and so I had all my walls painted in a bright shade of it. I saw a large floor lamp in the shape of a daffodil, and I had to have it. I bought action figures from TV shows of my youth and placed them in pride of place on my mantelpiece. I started to collect marbles again.

I realised that I was living my life backwards. I had to be a grown-up when I'd been a little boy, and now I was tending to the little boy inside who'd never had the chance to properly play. I didn't question it. I went with it. I liked it.

I am referred to often as having a childlike quality, or being pixielike. At first, when these sorts of descriptions began to be attributed to me, I didn't like them. Childhood for me had such negative connotations that the idea that I was in some way overly connected to that time in my life was a cause for concern, not celebration. *Why* was I so childlike? Was I in some way emotionally retarded, trapped, trying desperately to reconfigure my past before I could move on?

Eventually I began to feel more comfortable with it all. Childlike, I realised, tends to mean open, joyous, maybe a bit mischievous, and I am happy to have all those qualities. Had I not had the childhood I did, would these traits not be so at the forefront of my personality? Who knows? All I know is that I am the product of *all* the experiences I have had, good and bad, and if I am in a happy place in my life (as I truly am), then I can have no regrets about any of the combination of events and circumstances that have led me to the here and now.

When I joined Twitter I described myself as "Scottish elf trapped inside middle-aged man's body" and I still think that's accurate.

But that day as I ambled listlessly along the platform at King's Cross, I worried about how my father's latest intervention in my wellbeing might manifest itself. I had already reclaimed my lost childhood. What could happen now?

Minutes later I found myself at the cashier of a souvenir shop, buying a Noddy doll. Noddy and his friend Big Ears were characters invented by the beloved children's author Enid Blyton, whose books I had devoured as a boy.

The little boy was obviously still there . . .

I hope he never goes away.

THURSDAY 27TH MAY 2010

I woke up in Lille after another anxious night's sleep. I had eaten in my hotel room alone, the crew having had to go and get some location shots before the sun went down. As much as I knew it was necessary for me to have time on my own to process everything that was happening, and to allow myself the chance to give rein to my emotions, I also yearned for company. I Skyped with Grant back in London, which offered little relief. It was great to be able to see him, not just hear him, and for this I am grateful to modern technology. But at the same time, seeing the one you love but not being able to touch, when their comfort is what you crave most, actually makes you feel worse, and more depleted, than if you had not seen them at all. As Macbeth says, " 'Twas a rough night."

The next day I found myself waiting. As is usual in the film and television business, one spends a lot of time waiting for filming to begin. In this case, my location was a flat, open ploughed field between the villages of Violaine and La Bassée. I stood waiting for the crew to set up and make a plan of how to shoot the forthcoming revelation. I was asked to do endless walking shots, necessary for the potential voice-overs. All I wanted was to know what had made Tommy Darling such a hero, and I was standing next to a little historian who was itching to tell me, but of course nothing could be said until we were in the optimum position for the revelation to be revealed and my reaction properly captured.

I realised I was trapped in a sort of genealogical aspic, both in my real life and in my TV life. Both of us were being kept waiting for the truth.

All that was inscribed on Tommy Darling's medal was "Bravery in the Field", but it was becoming apparent that it was a much bigger deal than it sounded, what with the trip to Buckingham Palace and also the way the crew were whispering and preparing for the revelation I was about to hear.

Finally, this little historian, called David, was allowed off the leash. He began to tell me the story of the day my grandfather earned his medal. The 1st Cameron Highlanders, my grandfather's battalion, were defending La Bassée against the Germans. David pointed to the right, back along the road we had just driven up to get us to this field.

I could tell David was excited about the story, as excited as I was to hear it. He continued on, explaining where the Highlanders were based in Violaine, in relation to La Bassée. And that on that fateful day, the German general Rommel had directed his fleet of tanks across a canal and across the very fields we were standing on.

"There are about three hundred of them, and this is perfect tank country: it's flat, there is no cover."

I looked up. He was right. I could see for miles across the smooth plane of the French countryside.

My grandfather's role was to carry messages and orders from

the battalion base to the members of the company who were ahead, closer to battle in La Bassée. That day, David told me, my grandfather had done just that. But that wasn't all.

I could feel my pulse racing. It was faintly surreal to be standing in the mud, in northern France with a film crew and a little academic with regulation leather patches on the elbows of his tweed jacket, being handed an ancient tome that would reveal something so important about a blood relative I had never known. How did this become my life?

I began to read from the book David handed me. "'The forward Companies were supplied with ammunition and in one case with a Bren gun, by the work of 2928278 Lance Corporal T. Darling, who on his motorcycle, and laden with ammunition boxes and other necessities for the Companies in La Bassée, made repeated journeys from Violaine to La Bassée along the fire-swept road.'"

"For 'his gallantry and devoted conduct'," I continued reading, "'Lance Corporal Darling was recommended for, and later awarded, the Military Medal.'"

I looked up, awed.

The road behind us, David said, was most likely the very road that Tommy Darling had so bravely driven down. His bike, loaded with boxes of live ammunition, was a ready target for the German tanks. And yet Tommy Darling had kept going, fearlessly, to help his brothers in war.

"Had a bullet hit one of those boxes of ammunition," David said gleefully, "he would have probably gone up like a Roman candle."

Then he handed me the official citation, which explained exactly why Tommy Darling had been given his medal.

I read aloud once more: "'Lance Corporal Darling took forward on a motorcycle two Bren guns and a supply of ammunition as reinforcement. He carried out this hazardous and difficult operation under mortar and machine gun fire'!" At this last piece of information my voice trailed upward in disbelief.

"Whoa! It's like the *Commando* comics!" I joked, referencing the jingoistic Second World War comic books we had all been plied with in my youth. "Mein Gott! Gott im Himmel!"

I suddenly imagined that Tommy Darling might appear any second now, bursting through plumes of smoke from around the corner where the trees abutted the road, rounds of ammunition and guns strewn about him, tanks and snipers shooting at him as he sped by on his bike, a determined and heroic smile spread across his twenty-four-year-old face. I felt such a deep surge of sadness, just then, that I had never known this man. I suddenly realised. My grandfather was Steve McQueen!!

"He's so reckless!" I said aloud. I had no idea just *how* reckless Tommy Darling would eventually prove to be.

"He's reckless," David agreed. "I think he's also driven by two things."

"What are they?" I asked.

And then came the final blow, when David led me to the realisation that Tommy's battalion, the men he had thought of as his family for seven years at that point, were who he was risking his life for, and eventually that day, as the Germans surrounded the forward post, he must have realised there was nothing more he could do to help them.

"And they're trapped in La Bassée," I said, the full horror of the situation dawning on me.

"They're either trapped, or they're dead," David added bluntly.

I realised my grandfather and I had something in common. I too craved what I hadn't found in my childhood—security, approval, the love of my father—and throughout my adult life I have sought to re-create the experience of family. He seemed to be always in search of one, but now his actual family was many hundreds of miles away and his army family was literally dying all around him.

Despite his efforts and those of his fellow soldiers, German tanks quickly advanced on their positions and the regiment was split in two. More than three-quarters of them were trapped in La Bassée, where they were killed, captured, or went missing. Tommy Darling was one of the few who were left at battalion headquarters in Violaine. They retreated and were eventually evacuated from Dunkirk. Of the original eight hundred Cameron Highlanders who went to France, only seventy-nine answered the roll call when they returned to Britain.

It was time to leave the field and start the journey back to London. David talked a little more about the retreat to Dunkirk and the emotional and psychological toll it took on the men involved. One thing he said about my grandfather in particular stuck in my mind.

"He's probably wondering, *'Why me? Why did I get lucky?'*"

I began to feel I was at the scene of the beginning of the end of Tommy Darling.

On the train back to London, I thought constantly of my grandfather. He was becoming real to me. Not just a photograph on my hallway wall, but a man, my granddad. Someone who, had he lived, would have had a very big impact on my life. Someone I think I would have liked, and who, maybe, I was quite like myself.

"He's so reckless," I had said only this morning. And I began to think of how that word has often been used about me. I have a bit of the devil in me, you see. I am the one who wants to do

handstands at a party or take the shortcut down the dark alley
or jump into the roaring ocean after a few tequilas. Now, for the
first time in my life, I saw where all of that came from.

It was quite an eerie feeling to be recognising traits in myself
from a dead man.

I am lucky to have a partner who is a good counter to my recklessness. Sometimes Grant is the voice of reason, and talks me
down from doing something impetuous and, though fun, probably ill advised. Other times I poke him and remind him he's
being overcautious. I hoped my grandfather had someone in
his life like Grant. The recklessness he displayed on that road
in France was amazing, and rewarded with the highest accolade,
but ultimately it was for nought: he couldn't save his friends. I
worried that Tommy Darling was left with a distorted view of what
was worth risking his life for.

I also couldn't get a comment David had made about him out
of my mind.

"Why me?" he'd surmised my grandfather would have thought.

As a little boy I often wondered the same thing.

Why did my father hit me so much? What did I do to make him
so angry?

I came to believe that I, and my failings, were the cause of *all*
my life's woes: my father's rage, my parents' crumbling marriage,
my not being able to do anything right. The only time my father
even noticed me was when he hit me. Then, and the preceding
few moments, were the only time I knew I had the full focus of
his attention. But even as a little boy I knew that my association
of something so awful with my father's attention was unhealthy.
So then I began to feel guilty for thinking that way, and more
convinced it must be my fault that he hit me in the first place. It
was an easy spiral to observe from the future, but to a little boy

it seemed justified. My father loathed me, so it was only natural I should loathe myself.

My mother countered him, though. She told me I was special and loved. And actually, having two such opposing messages, although confusing, was ultimately pretty healthy. My father told me I was worthless, my mother that I was precious. They couldn't both be right, but they evened each other out and I began to make my own mind up, not just about myself but about everything that was going on around me. I think this was also good training for my future career. I didn't fully believe what either of my parents said about me, and I've taken that approach in dealing with critics of my work. "If you believe the good ones, you have to believe the bad ones" is my mantra. The most important opinion, of both my work and my conduct in life, is my own.

I looked at my watch. We still had a long way to go. I normally love a long train journey but not today. I began to wonder if my connection to Tommy Darling was just some pathetic attempt to lessen the blow of "losing" my father. It was certainly nice to have something else to think about. Every waking minute that I was not on camera was filled with questions about how I was going to navigate my future within my present family, and my potential new brood of relations, should they even want to acknowledge me. I kept thinking of the half brother my dad told me about. What was he like? Would we ever meet, ever be friends? And my new father, what would he feel about his new son being a celebrity, a famous actor now in need of fatherly love that he felt he had been denied? Did I even want that from him?

None of it could be resolved now. Not until the DNA test was done.

The kit had arrived the day before, and Tom had come up that afternoon and given a swab of his saliva. Now when I arrived back in London I would do the same, and we'd send it off to the lab and wait. We'd been told the results would be back in a few days, but that seemed so far away. However, I remembered that less than a week had passed since I'd been standing on that stage at the Hôtel du Cap, with a fuming Patti Smith, and I laughed at how fast life could carry you along. I tried to remember what I felt like back then, who I was even. So much had happened that I barely recognised myself in the pictures from that night, scrolling through them on my phone.

When I got home, the DNA test box was sitting on the dining table, waiting for me, like a lie detector test in some murder mystery movie. It scared me when I saw it. This was it, this was real, and this was definitive. I was taking a test to see if my father was telling the truth, and my mother had an affair, and I was the outcome. It seemed so crazy. Everything did, though. My life, pretty hectic and idiosyncratic on normal days, seemed utterly surreal now. I was moving through this moment as if I were trapped on one of those moving walkways that carry you through an aquarium, with sharks and manta rays gliding above and around you. I was in the middle of it all, unable to make it stop, and all I wanted to do was get home and stay there.

What I was about to do would either make it all stop, or unleash a whole new set of challenges. I would know if my father was telling the truth or not. I couldn't imagine why he would lie about this, but I also knew I had never been able to fully trust my father in my entire life. Regardless, the hardest, most upsetting part of knowing the truth was going to be telling my mother. Telling her I now knew the secret she had kept from me for forty-five years would be devastating for us both. I knew she would never do anything to hurt me, but I also knew she would be guilt-stricken by her own deceit. She must have had her reasons, I kept telling myself. And as much as I wanted to know them, I also never wanted to see my mother in distress again.

And what if it wasn't true? Where did that leave me then? What on earth would my father do when I confronted him with his lie? What if it wasn't a lie, but a misunderstanding? How would he treat me if he knew that this child he had tormented was indeed his son?

It was all just too much.

I put a swab of my saliva in a little test tube, put it in the box next to Tom's, and sealed it. Tomorrow morning it would be winging its way to some lab, and I would be winging my way to the Imperial War Museum to meet another boffin who was going to tell me the next instalment in my grandfather's wild ride through life.

Rather alarmingly, considering the fragile state of both my and Tommy Darling's psyches at this stage of our parallel stories, the Imperial War Museum is housed in the Bethlem Royal Hospital, also known as Bedlam, London's once notorious lunatic asylum.

THEN

When I was nineteen, my mother finally left my father.

I was in Glasgow in my final year at drama school, but had been allowed to leave for a term to make my professional theatre debut playing Malcolm in the Tron Theatre's production of *Macbeth*. On my twentieth birthday, my mum came down to Glasgow to see me and we had lunch and spent a pleasant afternoon together. Two days later I was surprised to hear her voice when I picked up the phone in my flat.

"Is everything okay, Mum?" I asked.

"Oh yes, pet. I'm just calling to tell you that as of the twenty-first of April I will be living at sixteen Brook Street, Monifieth."

There was silence on the line. I couldn't quite process what I'd heard.

"Um, what?" I managed finally.

"As of the twenty-first of April I will be residing at sixteen Brook Street, Monifieth," she repeated. "I've bought a wee flat and I get the keys in six weeks."

"What about Dad?" I asked, still confused.

"Oh, he'll be staying at Panmure."

"You're leaving him?"

"Well, Alan, you know your father and I have been leading separate lives for some time," I heard my little mum say.

Suddenly my legs gave way from under me and I was sitting on the floor crying like a baby. Of course I knew it was a positive thing for everyone concerned, especially my mum, but it really did come as a shock to me. I was terribly upset. Not so much about the actual break-up; more due to the recognition of how much of my youth had been spent vainly wishing for it to happen. The eventual announcement was more a ringing of the bell of grief from my childhood than the clanging of change in my present.

By this point, relations in the Cumming household were almost cordial. My parents seemed content in their separate lives, there seemed to be little animosity, and I assumed age had, if not withered, tempered my father's anger and lack of respect for his wife and family. Of course I later realised that this *détente* was due to a mutual agreement to eventually separate having been reached a couple of years before. At twenty I was deemed sufficiently capable to cope with the shock of having divorced parents.

A few weeks after my mother told me the news, I went to Panmure for the weekend. I realised this would be the last time I would ever sleep in my childhood home. There was no way I would return there except for a dutiful and cursory visit to see my father from then on. I would never again stay the night. Knowing this, I walked through the rooms and saw them in a new light. I was feeling nostalgic for something that had barely ended, perhaps because for so long I had yearned for it to cease.

I had already taken most of the things I wanted to keep when

I had first moved to Glasgow a couple of years earlier. For me that move was not just for a term, it was forever. I would return for visits at Christmas and the occasional weekend, but I was out, never to return for good. My mother, unbeknownst to me, was planning the same escape.

My mother took me to see her new flat, told me about the purchases she was making. I could see how excited she was for this new stage in her life. I understood.

My father was present for meals. He went out as usual for the evening, but he was not missed, and there was no malice or offence taken at his absence nor was his manner in any way aggressive or threatening as it had been for so many years. I interpreted this calmness as a good thing. Since I had gone off and begun to live my own life, my father had ceased to be a physical threat to me; he even became quite civil. This change in him allowed me to pack away much of my past in a box that I never wanted to open. For ten years I kept it closed, pretending that my family was no more difficult or trying than anybody else's. I didn't begin to forgive my father—far from it. But I began to forget him in a way, as I moved about the business of my future. My father had become not exactly jovial, but over a meal at the kitchen table I could tell him and my mum stories of my new, strange life at university and he would laugh. When he took me to the train station he would shake my hand and a ten- or a twenty-pound note would be passed into my palm and he would tell me to take it and buy myself and my mates a drink.

That last weekend, which had been so full of my mum's exhilaration and hope for the future, ended with a silent drive in my father's car to the train station at Dundee. He had not once mentioned or referenced the fact that Mum was leaving in a mere week or so. He had never voiced to me anything about how things might change. He had said absolutely nothing at all. My mum had spoken in front of him about some of the logistics of her move, but he showed no emotion or even interest. I suppose I felt sorry for him that weekend. I actually worried about him.

In the darkness of the car that Sunday night I eventually plucked up the courage to say, "Dad, we haven't talked at all about Mum leaving, and I'm just a bit worried about how you're going to get on, you know, look after yourself and everything. Don't you think you might need some help?"

Nothing. Not a malicious or pissed-off nothing, just *nothing*.

"I mean, don't you think you should maybe get someone to come and help you a bit," I continued. "To do some cooking and ironing and stuff?"

"I don't need anyone to do my cooking and ironing," came the enigmatic reply.

Little did I know then that as soon as my mother had packed up her car for the final trip to her new home and wished my father well, his lover—she of the suicide husband and the inappropriate autograph request at my granny's funeral—would be installed in her place. And so my father was right, he didn't need anyone to do his cooking or ironing.

FRIDAY 28ᵀᴴ MAY 2010

The next morning, when I arrived at the Imperial War Museum, I was introduced to Professor Edgar Jones, a historian and expert on military psychiatry. Of course I assumed that my grandfather must have suffered some psychological damage after such a traumatic experience in France—how could he not?—but the speed at which I was plunged into talking about his mental health made me rather anxious. I was just getting to know him, just scraping away at the picture in my hall and feeling real flesh and blood (and such derring-do!), and now I was being forced to chip away at his mind. In the place that had once housed England's mentally ill.

"War changes people," was Edgar's opening salvo.

He had a kind face. I had watched him talk to Elizabeth, the director, as the crew set up the lights, and I sensed that what he had to tell me did not sit easily with him. He was as uncomfortable as I was. They were looking through the medical journals and military documents spread out in front of them, speaking in whispers. Of course this was all so that my shock could be captured on camera, and I knew this. But the need for the secrecy, and the promise of shock, created a palpable sense of foreboding. Another day, another bombshell, I thought to myself.

The night before I had been happy to spend back at my flat with Grant, and I felt my batteries were a little recharged. On Sunday I would return to Cape Town in South Africa, where I would continue work on a mini-series I was acting in. Then there would be a month-long gap before I launched into the final piece of the Tommy Darling puzzle. I had said to Grant the night before that it was actually a good thing to have that expanse of time, as no doubt the results of the DNA test, which hopefully we would receive in a few days, would usher in a whole new level of family revelation and discussion. It would be nice to have just one of my familial mysteries to focus on for a while.

But as much as I longed for the answer, I knew that either way the DNA results would create emotional turbulence on a grand scale. If I was indeed not my father's son, I would have to confront my mother with the news and find out why she had kept this from me for so long. Then I would perhaps start the process of contacting my real father and new family. If it was not true, and my DNA completely matched Tom's, I would have to confront my father and once more engage with his warped and cruel mind, and also tell my mother what he had accused her of. Either way it looked like my mum was going to have the biggest shock of all of us—for she was at the centre of both scenarios. I just hoped that what I found out about her father was going to be more uplifting and positive than what I would find out about mine.

I let all thoughts of the next month go, and concentrated on what Edgar was telling me, which was essentially that there was no way my grandfather could have come through his war experience, and trauma, unscathed.

He went on to talk about how soldiers suffering from psychiatric problems during the Second World War were given rest, exercise and occupational therapy, but few were ever treated with what we would today call psychotherapy. Most cases, in fact, went untreated. Even the terms *"combat stress"* or *PTSD* (post-traumatic stress disorder) were relatively recent additions to the lexicon of war, and certainly not in the vocabulary in the 1940s. My grandfather had been fearless in battle, but he also had the weight of all he had seen to come to terms with later.

But worse was to come: if Tommy Darling had suffered mental trauma from his efforts in France, there would be little time for him to recover—in 1942 he and his fellow Cameron Highlanders were sent to India. There, the Highlanders found themselves tested in entirely new ways. They were trained in jungle warfare.

The Japanese had entered the war in 1941 after the bombing of Pearl Harbor, and very quickly developed a reputation for total lack of fear, and of fighting to the death. Edgar now pulled out a map and showed me that by March 1944 the Japanese forces had advanced through Burma and had their sights set firmly on neighbouring India, the jewel in the British Empire's crown. They crossed over the northeastern border and amassed their troops around the mountain town of Kohima with the aim of pushing west to take Delhi. I had a feeling this was not going to end well.

The Cameron Highlanders were on the front lines of the battle at Kohima, made to push through Japanese forces that had taken positions on a hillside. The Highlanders fought mortar fire, grenades, snipers . . . all with the knowledge that the Japanese took no prisoners. To be caught was to be killed.

He paused for a moment and I took out the Officer's Record

of Service of Tommy Darling, a book that my mum had given me earlier in the week. I had studied it carefully for any clues.

In the book I had found that my grandfather had been admitted to a hospital after this battle, on May 18, 1944. Next to the entry were three letters.

"What does this mean, G.S.W.?" I asked.

"It's a general acronym for gunshot wound," explained Edgar.

The entry also said "left hand", "right knee", and "ankle", which meant, according to Edgar, that Tommy Darling had most likely been hit by shrapnel. His wounds weren't clean.

My stomach lurched a bit. What a horrible image.

The book Mum had given me also showed us that two weeks after he was wounded in the Battle of Kohima, Tommy Darling was admitted to a hospital in Dehra Dun, northwest of Kohima. Seven months later, in December 1944, he was moved to another hospital in Deolali, almost a thousand miles away, where he stayed for two months before returning to duty.

Why had he been moved such a huge distance in the middle of his recovery?

There was a gap in the book, from May 1944 to 1946. I knew that the key to the mystery of Tommy Darling lay in those missing two years.

"What does that mean?" I asked immediately. Edgar looked at me with his soulful eyes and said, "It's possible these records may have been deliberately destroyed. We can't be sure."

And so, with Edgar's urging, I went back to the previous entry. Tommy had left the hospital in Dehradun and was transferred to Deolali.

"And you may have heard of the word 'doolally', which derives from Deolali. We've been wondering whether, in fact, he goes to a psychiatric ward within the general hospital at Deolali."

Oh, poor, wee doolally Tommy Darling.

Doolally was a word I used all the time in my childhood. Even now, occasionally I fire it off. I had no idea its provenance was a hospital in India, and I certainly never imagined it would be used to describe my granddad.

It all started to click into place.

I could feel poor Edgar's conundrum—his human reluctance to give me more bad news battling his academic needs to complete the theory, tell me the rest of the story.

"Two terrible battles, possibly one of the most frightening engagements of the Second World War, followed by severe wounds . . . ," Edgar let out, slowly.

And there it was. Tommy Darling, the fearless daredevil of war on two continents, who had seen his fellow soldiers, no, his family, die around him, had slipped through the cracks of sanity and gone under.

And in the Second World War, that wasn't acknowledged, or discussed. Suddenly a lightbulb went on for me. "That makes more sense about why they'd destroy those medical records then, doesn't it?"

"These records were systematically destroyed after the Second World War if someone had a major psychiatric admission, because of the stigma attached to mental illness."

I suddenly felt a rush of animosity towards the military establishment, towards a country that sent its poor young men to war and let their brains become addled only to destroy any record of such damage, thereby heaping shame back onto the very young men who had given and lost so much in the first place. No wonder there is still such stigma today.

THEN

When I was twenty-eight I had what I have come to describe as a nervous breakdown. I now see that it had been coming for years—wobbly moments of irrationality and panic, which I had chalked up to exhaustion or stress, now can be traced to the path that led me to the eventual Nervy B.

I think about it as that box in my attic. Our parents' house was a silent one. Partly that was due to not wanting to risk the ire of our father, and so not speaking at all was a safer option. But also we never discussed what we were going through, how it was affecting us. When my dad was absent, sometimes Mum, Tom and I would give each other warnings over what might ignite his rage, or express anger about the consequence of one of his actions, or indirectly empathise about our plight, but we never actually addressed what was really going on: that we were living with a tyrant, someone who, I believe now, was mentally ill. As our silence grew, so did our denial.

Eventually of course we all escaped him. Tom and I entered adulthood and moved away: Tom at twenty-one to get married, and I, two years later at seventeen, to go to drama school in Glasgow. And Mary Darling started her own independent life soon after. We all stitched together facades that we were all okay. Fine. Normal. Of course we weren't. You can't go through sustained cruelty and terror for a large swathe of your life and not talk about it and be okay. It bites you on the arse big time.

Tom and I are six years apart in age. That doesn't seem to matter now, but when I was ten and he was sixteen it was huge. And when I was fifteen and he was twenty-one and he got away, I was devastated, not so much because I was losing the brother I had shared a bedroom with for so many years, for in truth we didn't have all that much in common and weren't that close then, but because I was being left alone and there was no longer any buffer between my father's rage and me.

Later, when we were older, we'd occasionally broach the topic of our past when drunk with friends and the subjects of parents and childhoods came up. But Tom and I would do so in a sort of jokey way, marvelling at the impossible tasks our father would set for us, and the times he had become really enraged, never detailing the violence or the fear he also engendered.

So the box in the attic stayed up there, gathering dust, neglected. Eventually I think we forgot about it completely. But the thing about boxes full of denial and years of unresolved pain and hurt is that eventually . . . they explode.

My box began to burst in 1993. I had been married to my wife for seven years and we had decided to try to have a baby. Suddenly the idea of being a father and what that actually means began to fill my head, and therefore my own experiences with my father flooded my mind. Not vividly and truthfully for a long time, though, for I had packed them away so well that it took a long time for the gates to open and the trickle to turn into a flood.

At first all that happened was that I started to panic. I put it down to the fact that my wife and I were moving into a big new house and the financial demands that suddenly made on me. Then we had a problem with our next-door neighbour, and I thought perhaps that was the cause. The house had a huge garden and I threw myself into its restoration, but many serene moments were ruined when I was hard at work digging or hacking away at brambles and I would feel that my wife was watching me. Suddenly I couldn't carry on. I became agitated and irritable. I realised that her innocently looking out of the kitchen window, or standing at the top of the lawn, sometimes even bringing me a drink or coming for a chat, triggered the feeling of my father inspecting me. As I weeded the seedbeds in the nursery, or as I cleaned out the tractor shed, I remembered being watched, and my whole body, my *being*, just associated that gaze with the inexorability of being hit. My wife knew my father and we had visited him a few dutiful times over the years, but she had no idea of the scope of his abuse and his power over me. I explained my feelings of discomfort and she was very understanding. She stopped watching me.

Then, around the same time, I began rehearsals to play *Hamlet*. It was to tour England, culminating in a month-long run at the Donmar Warehouse in London. It was the most amazing and challenging moment of my career thus far. My wife was playing Ophelia, so she would be with me every step of the way. As I got deeper and deeper into my work, I came to understand that Hamlet really didn't want to be there. He wanted to be absent. He wanted to be back at university with his friends. He is sickened with his mother's hasty marriage, distraught to be asked by the ghost of his father—a distant man I thought he didn't particularly connect with—to avenge his death. To add to it, his girlfriend is dumping him and his friends are spying on him. I decided that there was no way Hamlet was mad. He was slipping into the same deep water as me. He was at the start of a nervous breakdown too.

Spending so much time thinking about the concepts of being a father and being a son and trying to interpret the slow trickle of memories and feelings about my own silent childhood soon made it very difficult for me to engage with my friends in the cast. I was also exhausted of course—*Hamlet* is a huge undertaking—but I began to use my fatigue and also the need for solitude to prepare for the performances to cover up what was an actual inability to think about anything else. I pushed my friends, and my wife, far away.

I began to wonder what kind of father I would be. I had seen and read enough about psychology to worry whether I would just *become* my father, and the more I allowed myself to remember what that actually was, the more anxious I became. What had he actually done? He was just a bit strict and prone to losing his temper, wasn't he? He hit me sometimes, but everyone's dad hits them, don't they? He told me I was useless and worthless, but I have proved him wrong, haven't I? I was okay.

I wasn't like him. I was kind, I loved kids, I wasn't an angry person. I was a different man. I would break the cycle.

Thinking back to this time, I truthfully don't think I remembered any of the actual details of my father's abuse. I was still in denial, along with my mother and Tom. Fear and silence will ensure that.

But as the months went by, I was becoming more and more ill-tempered, irrational and unable to communicate. The play was incredibly emotional and exhausting of course, but I knew it wasn't just that. My wife and I were still trying for a child, but I was secretly becoming more and more relieved each month when we hadn't been successful. Ironically, my career was taking off in a way I could never have imagined. I began rehearsals to play the Emcee in *Cabaret* during the day, whilst performing *Hamlet* at night. It was creatively amazing, but I was feeling more unhappy, anxious and out of control than I ever had in my life. Here I was, the bright new London theatre star, playing Hamlet alongside his wife's Ophelia, about to start a family. I had everything going for me, and I felt I had no control over anything.

I began to stop eating. I was pretty thin as it was, from doing the play, but I began to get perverse pleasure from eating as little as I could throughout the day. I even began to be fascinated by people noticing and worrying about my weight. Of course these are classic symptoms of an eating disorder, using food and your relationship to it as a smokescreen to avoid dealing with what really is the problem, but also feeling that by depriving your body you are at least in control of *something* in your life.

I cried a lot during this time. Deciding what to wear in the morning would set me off. Of course my wife was becoming more and more anxious, and annoyed, by the way I was seemingly unable to enjoy what should have been a blissful time for us both. When *Cabaret* began, I was with a new group of people who didn't know me, and that helped. But at home I was an utter mess. I remember one evening when a group of my very close friends came to see the show, and we went for dinner after. They were shocked at my weight of course. I sat at the end of the table not talking to anyone, picking at a salad. I had forgotten how to be me. Like Hamlet, I wanted to be absent.

I wasn't yet able to recall details from my childhood. Instead, it was as if I were reliving the pain and the sadness I had felt as a child. I was doing this in an environment and at a time of my life that had no correlation to such pain, or to the behaviour it manifested in me. I couldn't understand why I was so sad. I just knew I needed to be away and to have some time on my own to sort myself out. I finally told my wife I didn't think I was ready to have a child. Understandably she was distraught and angry. I understood, but I couldn't verbalise sufficiently or logically why I had changed my mind. I began to wonder if I even wanted to stay in my marriage. I was unfit to be a father. I was unfit to be a husband.

By the time *Cabaret* ended in the spring of 1994, I was a zombie. I went to work, but I spent most days in bed if I had no appointments. I was in a deep depression. I knew that my depression was due to my past, and my father, but I just didn't dare to delve any deeper into it because I was afraid I would be utterly unable to function. I needed to get completely away.

I was offered a film in Ireland, and I leapt at the chance. Suddenly I was away from London, away from my crumbling marriage, living in an old abbey in the middle of County Kilkenny, with yet another bunch of people who knew nothing about me. This gave me the ability to have time to myself to think and to *sort myself out.* That was the phrase I kept hearing, kept repeating to myself. *You have to sort yourself out, Alan. By such and such a date you need to have sorted yourself out.*

The movie was *Circle of Friends,* and became a very happy respite from my funk. But I didn't sort myself out. I thought a lot. I wrote down a lot. I tried to figure things out and work out what I wanted. I felt so much pressure to pretend I was getting better, but I wasn't. The best thing was I got some rest, the desire to eat again, and the realisation that it was going to take more than a couple of months away making a film to sort myself out.

When I got back to London I moved out of my marital home and took a little flat in Primrose Hill. I stopped working. Now I would really *sort myself out.* It was a miserable little place I moved to, and I think that was intentional. I wanted no distractions. I wanted it just to be me with my memories, and of course now, finally, the box in my attic exploded.

FRIDAY 28TH MAY 2010, EARLY AFTERNOON

As soon as we left the Imperial War Museum, we went to lunch. We ate at the National Film Theatre café, and I recalled all the times I had eaten there during my time living and working in London. One evening, shortly after my run of *Hamlet* had concluded, when I was very deep in my descent into despair, I introduced the movie of Richard Burton's Broadway version of *Hamlet*. It's never good to see another version of something you've just finished, I realised that night. You either say the lines along with whoever is playing your part and are taken back into a black hole of your own interpretation and miss what you are watching entirely; or, as I did that night, you become rather irritable with the seemingly obvious and myriad flaws that you are witnessing! For me, never had there been so much irony as when Mr Burton said to the players, "Speak the speech, I pray you, . . . trippingly on the tongue!"

I also thought of the times I had spent working at the Royal National Theatre next door, and of late-night drunken walks along the banks of the Thames with a man I now realised had been the latest in a line of lovers I had engaged with because I was drawn to their anger and I wanted to fix them.

Just as when I was a little boy dealing with my father, I thought it must be my fault my lovers were so angry. Now, of course, I can see that it was stupid, irrational, and self-abusive to think so, but it was still a hard habit to kick.

My reverie was broken with some extraordinary news. Elizabeth showed me an e-mail from the Burma Star Association, a veterans' organisation they had contacted. It told me that they had found someone who remembered my grandfather.

"'David Murray is a veteran of the Battle of Kohima, where he fought with Thomas Darling,'" I read aloud from the e-mail. "'He's happy to meet with you and tell you what he remembers about him.'"

For the umpteenth time that week I was sideswiped. I never imagined that there would be anyone alive who remembered my granddad. The thought had never occurred to me.

But there was, and that very afternoon we set off for Bristol to meet David, who was now eighty-nine. Not only had this man known Tommy Darling, he had fought alongside him as his superior.

A few hours later we arrived in a very pleasant gated community overlooking the Bristol Sound. David was a spry old man with a twinkle in his eye. He was wearing a navy blue Cameron Highlanders sweatshirt, and evidence of his army days was everywhere around his apartment. Photographs, both of his days in service and of battalion reunions, decorated the walls. He was obviously a soldier through and through. I wondered how he would take to the line of questions I wanted to ask him, and particularly in reference to my granddad's mental health. First, though, he had another surprise for me . . .

"He was called Big Tam! He was tall for that time!" said David chirpily.

"He was called Big Tam?" I repeated in wonder.

"Oh yes, Big Tam, Big Tam Darling. Yes!"

His lovely, eager, smiley face beamed back at me. He was clearly enjoying his reminiscences.

"He was looked up to, as a—" I began.

"I looked up to him," he interrupted. "Oh yes, and everyone my age looked up to him. A man like that who had been in battle, who had been decorated for gallantry, and who had the service. Certainly one respected him. Men like him taught us our jobs. They were the backbone of the battalion at that time."

He paused, looking out the window at the setting sun.

"Nobody ever argued with Tom Darling," he added respectfully.

David told me of a man who was strong, tough, someone you never talked back to. And yet, despite his imposing stature and experience, he was a kind man too. David regaled me with stories of the jokes my grandfather would play, all the while keeping the men in his command aware that he was their leader. We then began to talk about the Battle of Kohima, which they had fought in together.

David's tone changed as he remembered the events of that awful night, how the men went up that hill to face the Japanese, single file and nearly silent because of their expert training. Four hundred Highlanders made it up that hill, waiting to strike.

I asked where my grandfather was at the time, leaning on the edge of my seat to take in every single word.

"Well, Tam was with the carrier patrol, and they were with the forward troops. As the darkness fell, the Japanese guns opened up on us, and it was a real war scene." Despite the inherent horror he was describing, David was almost smiling as he retold this story, clearly in his element and filled with pride at what he had been capable of, all those years ago.

"The Naga huts were blazing, the guns were firing, the smaller arms were popping away, my mortar was thudding away in the background. That night, a thunderstorm broke out, and about half past two in the morning, there was a flash of lightning, a roar of thunder, and out of the ground came two companies of Japanese, shrieking their heads off.

"It was the most unearthly sound I've ever heard in my life. *Tenno heika banzai!* May the emperor live a thousand years!"

It was terrifying. By the end, the Cameron Highlanders had lost a hundred and five of the four hundred men who had silently climbed that hill. A fourth of the battalion was dead, wounded, or simply missing.

David told me that Tam must have been wounded that night, for it was some time before he saw him again.

"The next time I saw him was in the aid post," David said. "The rain had started, we had lost a lot of men, we'd bitten off more than we could chew for a wee while. And everyone was a bit . . . realistic about things."

He paused, and I knew that euphemism was really a description of the deep gloom that must have descended on the battalion.

"And he had been affected, Tam had been affected." By the look in his eyes I knew he was trying to shield me from the true horror of just how much my grandfather had been *affected*.

"Do you think that he was having some sort of combat stress? I just sense that he had—"

Before I could continue, something in David's face changed

and he lurched forward in his chair for a second, then caught himself and leaned back.

"I just checked myself from contradicting you," he began, and I could swear there was a tear in his eye. He took a moment and swallowed.

"Nobody had heard of combat stress . . . in those days, sixty-five years ago now . . ."

"Yes, a long time," I interrupted nervously.

"It was a different generation, we were different men, this was a different country."

He looked at me sadly, through his steel-rimmed glasses, no longer the soldier filled with pride recalling his acts of bravery.

"I never thought that I had any combat stress. But when I was first married, my wife woke me up and said, 'What are you shouting for Sergeant Barrett for?' And he was my old platoon sergeant, the first name I always shouted."

He bit his lip and rested his head to one side for a moment.

"And my little daughter came up behind me when I was kneeling down doing something in the house and she said, *'Boof!'* And she said I turned around and she knew I could've killed her."

I sat in silence. There was no way this man could know the extent of what he had done for me that day. To say that I was thankful, in awe even, didn't do it justice.

David looked me deep in the eyes.

"He was a good man. He was one of the men that I respected. I did respect your grandfather."

"Thank you," I said, fighting back my tears.

THEN

At the top of our house at Panmure there was a room called the "Big Room". It was where Tom and I did our homework and played games. In the centre of the room there was a table where we played Ping-Pong. Once Tom had gone off to live with his wife, it became my hiding place. I would contemplate my future, gazing out at the endless rolling fields of the estate that sloped down to the North Sea. It was also where our deep freeze was, so my mum would make sporadic visits upstairs to get some food item or to deposit a Tupperware container of leftovers. But mostly, that room was my domain.

The Big Room was symbolic of so many things for me. It meant great solace on the nights when I'd go there to hide and avoid my father's rage, listening to Kate Bush albums and plotting my eventual escape. I remember so vividly when the prospectus of the Royal Scottish Academy of Music and Drama arrived and I took the first glimpses at the place that was to become my sanctuary. I studied hard at my schoolwork in that room too, rallying myself to be more focused and intent, with the notion that every minute of study represented an hour or a day of freedom in my not-too-distant future.

One night, my father pierced through the walls of my asylum. It was the night before my music O-Grade exam. I was doing well in the subject, but like any hardworking, anxious student, I was spending the night before a big final test cramming and going over the previous year's notes to make sure I was completely prepared.

At about 7:30 P.M. my father threw open the door to the Big Room, and stood behind me. My desk was in the window that overlooked the nursery and our field, which was presently bereft of sheep and so had been mowed.

"The field's been mowed," my father said in that dark, inevitable way, and I knew this was not going to end well.

I turned round to look at him. Surely he wasn't going to . . . not tonight of all nights.

"I have my O-Grade music tomorrow," I said pleadingly.

"Never mind that," he said, already turning for the door and his bedroom where he would change and then leave for the evening, to drink in the local pub or entertain one of his women.

"Get down to that field and rake up that grass!"

And he was gone.

"I have to study!" I shouted after him. These days my burgeoning teenage manhood made me put up a bit of a, if not fight, then at least protest.

"Get it done," he thundered. And I knew I had no choice. I would have to forgo my last-minute studying and spend the evening raking an entire field's worth of grass. It was as if my father had been reading my mind and knew that I had come to view school as my first step towards freedom. It couldn't have been more of a conscious action on my father's part. He wanted me to fail.

I did the raking, eventually having to do so by flashlight as the sun went down. I knew the consequences of that field not being cleared by the time I left for school the next morning were inconceivable. I ran for the bus with blistered hands as my father silently inspected me across the sawmill yard. I felt like I might never get away.

That night I got home and he asked me how my exam had gone. I knew I had done well, but I didn't want to give him that knowledge. I didn't want to let him ever think he was justified. I never did. Instead, I became that much more driven to succeed.

Hanging in one of the cupboards of the Big Room was the uniform my father had kept from his days in the Air Force: a blue, thick wool, itchy pair of baggy trousers and a short jacket. There was also a long, grey raincoat, which he said he had worn when he first returned to 'Civvy Street' or the real world as referred to by the young men in the British forces. When I left home to go to university, I took these items of my father's, along with a blue tank top my mum had knitted for him. I didn't ask if I could have them, for I knew what the answer would be. So I stole them.

I'm still not sure why I did this. It was the early eighties and everyone was wearing baggy, vintage ensembles, but that wasn't the whole reason. In some way, I suppose the clothes came to represent my relationship with my dad. I needed a piece of him, something more than bad memories and pain. I needed him to know that I could take too, even if it was only things, and not innocence, or childhood. And also they meant it wasn't over. It wouldn't be resolved for many years to come.

Over the years I lost or gave away the army ensemble and eventually the grey raincoat, but never the knitted blue tank top. It is upstairs in a cupboard in my house. I haven't worn it for decades, but I see it every now and then as I reach for things on the high shelf it sits on. Occasionally I take it down and smell it, imagining I can still feel him, or in some way Panmure and that time of my life. I realised recently that I wore it in the first headshots I had taken when I was starting out as an actor. I think I needed to remind myself that wherever my future might take me, it was important never to forget where I'd come from. That sweater is still a portal to another time, another life, yet it is a part of my happiness today, because it's a part of me.

SATURDAY 29TH MAY 2010

I woke up the next morning with a hangover. I had gone out with the crew in Bristol the night before, and lots of beer and hardly any water was partaken of. Everyone it seemed was up for a big night. I was sharing one of the most revelatory and mind-blowing weeks of my life with relative strangers, but even so, these men and women were almost as emotionally invested in my granddad's story as I was. It made for a good amount of camaraderie, and certainly gave me a chance to forget about everything else going on in my life at that moment.

We drove back to London on Saturday morning and I thought about all I had learned about Tommy Darling. I decided my grandfather was still Tommy to me. He may have been Tam to David and to the men who looked up to him in his battalion, but I knew his secrets, and he would remain forever Tommy. Tommy was a great, respected and decorated soldier, but also a daredevil, a cheeky chap, and in search of something. Was it family? Was it thrills? Maybe it was both. It was certainly belonging. And I understood that. I also understood how events or circumstances could cascade out of control and your entire ability to deal with the present can be lost.

When we reached London we headed for a street just off Piccadilly where, in a very stuffy military officers' club, I was to see yet another historian. Rob Liman was going to tell me about Tommy Darling's life after the war.

I learned from Rob that after his stint in the hospital at Deolali, Tommy Darling returned to duty in India for the remaining months of the war. In 1945 he returned to Britain to visit his wife and family. But that was the last time they would ever see him.

He was made an officer and stayed in the army for four more years, working in an administrative role in Germany and the UK, close to his family and yet never visiting home. Earlier in the week I had seen, on one of the many documents that had been presented to me, a contact address for Tommy Darling during a period of leave he had from the army, in St Albans. This was puzzling. My granny and my mum and uncles were hundreds of miles away at the top of Scotland. Why had my grandfather lived in St Albans? Why did he never go home?

I also knew that my granddad had ended his life in Malaysia, formerly Malaya, working for the Malayan police force, but why he had taken a job so far away from home was also a mystery. Rob, a dashing, natty, signet-ring-wearing military type, was dying to explain why.

My grandfather had seen a flyer advertising jobs as lieutenants in the Malaysian police force. He was attracted to the chance to see more of the world, to reclaim some of the excitement of war. He was still a young man, with years ahead of him.

"It just so happens," Rob said, "that we have managed to find a copy of his application form."

He handed it to me and I began to read aloud.

"'Surname: Darling. Christian name: Thomas. Whether single, married, or a widower: Ma—'"

I looked along to the end of the line and was completely shocked.

Tommy Darling's answer to his marital status was "Married (Separated)".

What did that mean?

"Separated!" I repeated. "Why does my mum not know that?"

Immediately I thought of my having to call Mary Darling, who had been so eager for any tidbit I had sent her over the last week. Now I would be the one to tell her that her parents were, in fact, separated when her father went to Malaysia.

Rob said nothing. The room was silent except for my breathing. I took a deep breath and sighed it out.

"Well, that makes sense," I eventually said.

This was why Tommy Darling had never returned to Scotland. This was why he had gone halfway around the world, disappearing forever.

Rob went on to tell me that the issue of soldiers being separated from their wives and families back home was a big concern during the war. There was a lot of talk about how this affected the morale of the men at the front.

The next line of the form revealed another clue to the mystery. When asked for the number of his children, Tommy had written three. Two sons and one daughter. But he had *three* sons. My uncle Raymond was the youngest child and was not mentioned on this form. Maybe he was born after this? But no, I knew he had been born in 1942, and Tommy Darling had filled in this application form I was now reading seven years later, in 1949. They were separated, and Raymond was not listed as being the son of Tommy Darling . . . It all came into focus.

I looked up at Elizabeth, the director, who was looking back at me apologetically. Immediately I knew.

"So Raymond was not his son?" I asked incredulously. "My gran had a child out of wedlock?"

The parallels of our two stories were running unnervingly closer and closer.

"There was no name listed under Father on Raymond's birth certificate," Elizabeth said softly.

I have now discovered something that my granny did, unbeknownst to her daughter. This is the very same daughter who, according to my father at least, had done exactly the same thing. Honestly, I was too shocked to form words. I let Rob do all the talking.

He told me that Tommy Darling continued sending money back home, but never once visited. By the time he filled in this application form for the job in Malaysia, the one I was holding, he hadn't seen his children for almost four years.

I joked with Rob that every time he opened his mouth I was afraid there would be some new family revelation. I wasn't sure I could handle another one.

There was no way of knowing exactly when my grandparents had split up, or even if my granny's pregnancy with my uncle Raymond was the cause of it. Perhaps they had parted amicably, beforehand. There certainly doesn't seem to have been any record of animosity between them, in either the letters and papers that the researchers unearthed or in the legacy of how he was perceived in my family. But whatever the circumstances, they can only have added to Tommy Darling's isolation and his feelings of loss and dispossession. After he left the army he made a new life for himself in St Albans, working in an auto and motorcycle parts shop, but less than a year later he gave it all up and entered a war zone once more. Clearly he was drawn to the drama of battle. Civilian life didn't suit him, certainly not once his marriage had ended and his wife had moved on.

So Tommy Darling was a lifelong soldier? Maybe the horrors he had encountered in his career were so ingrained in him that he could no longer function unless he had access to their potential.

But whatever the reasoning, he was about to walk into the middle of the most brutal of colonial wars.

Malaya, or Malaysia as it is now known, was bordered to the north by Thailand and in turn is just a bridge's distance north of the island of Singapore. It had been part of the British Empire since the early nineteenth century, and its huge rubber and tin resources made it a hugely valuable asset to the UK.

But after the Second World War, Malaya saw growing unrest as its economy suffered, and soon the Malayan National Liberation

Army, the military arm of the Malayan Communist Party, began a campaign to disrupt British trade in an attempt to overthrow its colonial rule. In 1948 three European plantation managers were murdered and what became known as the Malayan Emergency began. (Actually the Malayans called it the "Anti-British National Liberation War", but the rubber and tin companies used the term "*emergency*" because they would not have been able to claim for any losses from Lloyds of London had the term "*war*" been used. Cheeky, right?)

In order to fight back at the guerrillas and allow the rubber plantations to continue production, the British government set up villages to house their workers, protected by barbed wire fences and accessible only through checkpoints. But not only were the workers protected, these villages also ensured that the Communist insurgents were cut off from them, and from any food or supplies they might try to pass on. Nearly half a million people were forced to move into these villages, and though many were happy to be protected from the guerrillas, there were also many who were secretly Communist sympathisers.

So as if the threat of execution from irate young Communist vigilantes was not enough, Tommy Darling would also have to constantly look over his shoulder in case of attack from the very people he was paid to protect—the Malayan workers.

Tommy was in an incredibly difficult, dangerous situation. He had to win the confidence of the locals so that they wouldn't betray him to the Maoists. He also had to protect these very same people from constant threat of insurgent attack. Many British officers who went to Malaya were killed.

So was this how Tommy Darling met his fate? Was the "shooting accident" my mother spoke of a military euphemism for some bleak, bloody political sacrifice?

What was even more galling to think was that a mere seven months after taking up his post in Malaya, Tommy Darling would be dead, at only thirty-five years of age.

This was the point of the story where I had been warned that Rob could say no more. The next week of filming, commencing in a month's time, would take me to Malaysia, where I would find out the truth about my granddad's death.

I said my good-byes to the crew and decided to walk home through Soho to my flat, in an attempt to clear my head. I had invited a few friends to come over for a little party that night and I just needed some time alone to let everything sink in before I donned the facade of normality that I needed to wear for the evening.

What I couldn't stop thinking about was the similarities between the story that was unfolding on TV and the real one I was experiencing off camera. Both my mother and my grandmother had a child out of wedlock. I could understand how dented Tommy Darling must have been at receiving that news because I had received such news just days before myself—though Tommy and I had very different perspectives. I was the child of such a union. Tommy was the scorned husband.

On a more visceral level, I realised we had both suffered from a form of post-traumatic stress disorder. We both had gone under, slipped through the net for a while, and we both perhaps enjoyed the thrill of danger and excitement because we had at one time cheated death, or quivered at the very edge between it and life.

I got home and broke down in tears. I was totally exhausted. This week had been the most insane of my entire life. Now, for the first time since this all started, I was able to let go and breathe a sigh of relief because I knew I wouldn't have to gird my loins for any more revelations, at least for a day or two. The DNA test results would arrive back in London the following week, but by then I would be in Cape Town filming that mini-series. Tomorrow I would call my mum and tell her about her parents' separation and Raymond's birth certificate, but for tonight, at least, I was a free man. And tonight, as though the showbiz gods could tell that I needed levity and sparkle and wacky Euro froth, was the night of the Eurovision Song Contest!!

Most Americans of course have never heard of this great institution, and I can only feel sorry for them. I know this because I spent almost all my down time between takes in the movie *Spy Kids* playing Eurovision trivia with Antonio Banderas, much to the bemusement of the crew in Austin, Texas. They looked at us as though we were members of a cult, and in a way, we are. It is part of my pop DNA, it is a rite of passage, a touchstone, and eventually it transcends its awful shallow shininess to become a communal nostalgic shrine to which we make our annual drunken pilgrimages. It's like Christmas or Thanksgiving but without the family feuds and with a pretty racy bpm. I grew up with it, and I will almost certainly die with it, or perhaps *from* it. It gave us *ABBA,* people!! Celine Dion won in 1988, representing *Switzerland*!!

I have often thought that if Americans were more exposed to this wonder there would not only be a huge surge in their understanding of British wit and irony, but they would perhaps be able to appreciate without shame the value of a good old-fashioned tacky pop song. I feel my American friends are so very worried about seeming gauche or vulgar when it comes to pop music. It's only when certain styles of music are placed within the ironic context of *retro* that Americans can fully enjoy them. We Europeans have never had that problem. Sometimes the lowest common denominator is a positive thing, and people can bond over their love of pop trash.

As we prepared for the party, and the stress of my genealogical maelstrom slowly trickled away, I began to worry that perhaps the Eurovision Song Contest had changed. I had often tried to describe to Grant just how monumental a cultural institution it was, but we'd never been in the UK together when it was on so I had never fully succeeded. YouTube clips are all very well, but they don't allow for the sense of occasion, the sense of international rivalry, the tension of the juries' pronouncements, and the sheer joy of hearing bad pronunciation of English over a Europoppy beat.

Perhaps I was over-romanticising its surreal qualities. Perhaps Europe had become more sophisticated in its musical tastes, and tonight's great expectations would fall a little flat.

I needn't have worried. It was a vintage year. For example, Armenia's entry was a haunting power ballad entitled "Apricot Stone", about . . . apricot stones!

During Spain's rendition of "Algo Pequenito" ("Something Tiny") there was a stage invasion and a man in a funny hat ran on and joined in with the dancers who were dressed as clowns and dolls. Had it not been for the bouncers racing onstage to remove him I doubt the rest of Europe would have realised this was not rehearsed, but because of this insult to their finely honed performance, something unprecedented happened and Spain was allowed to perform *again* at the end of the contest! Perhaps they shouldn't have, though, as sadly this double exposure did little to help their fortunes and they ended up in fifteenth place.

My personal favourite was the Belarus entry, "Butterflies", which, two-thirds of the way through, perfectly blended the aural and visual when butterfly wings sprouted from the backs of the three female band members' gowns just as the song edged up a dutiful semitone and one of the boys started a Mariah Carey-style cadenza.

Who knew that it would take the Eurovision Song Contest to make me level, to balance the week I had endured, to allow me to revivify my spirit and feel I could take on whatever demons were soon destined to cross my path?

MONDAY 31ST MAY 2010

I landed in Cape Town early after flying through the night from London. It was such a relief to be back at work, to have something else to think about.

The previous afternoon I had called my mum and told her the news about her parents having separated and her brother Raymond not being Tommy Darling's son. She admitted that she was not entirely shocked by the news, which gave me some comfort, I suppose. Over the years she had entertained many possibilities of why her father hadn't been around, and rumours had long circulated within the family about her brother.

"It's just good to know the truth, though, isn't it, Alan?" she said. "To have everything cleared up."

"Yes, I really think it is, Mum," I replied. There was another truth that I knew would be good for me to hear. The results of the DNA test were due in a few days. The wait was killing me. Going back to work and having a complete change of scene was probably the best thing for me. After I spoke to Mum, and said my good-byes to Grant, who was returning to New York, I left for Heathrow and my next few weeks in South Africa.

I love long flights. The feeling of being completely unreachable is something I savour, and the limbolike state of being, having departed but not arrived, somehow allows me to catch up with myself, to regroup and check in. It's a little contrary to think that I look forward to careering through the skies in a metal-fatigued box in order to gain some feeling of inner calm, but that's the way I roll.

But there are other ways my emotions are thrown into flux at thirty-nine thousand feet. Films I would never otherwise have watched suddenly seem very alluring and then render me a weeping wreck. Around that time I remember they all tended to have Sandra Bullock in them. I cry a lot on planes. This flight was no exception.

I was returning to South Africa because I was in the middle of shooting a television mini-series called *The Runaway*, based on the novel by Martina Cole. It was set in London's seedy Soho streets in the sixties and seventies, and I played Desrae, a transvestite who runs the Peppermint nightclub, and who takes in the eponymous runaway and becomes her matriarchal figure. Desrae was a survivor, literally, for there were more than a few gangland shoot-outs peppered throughout the six episodes (including one that ended with my Italian gangster boyfriend being gunned down, and dying in my arms!) and she also was a really kind, dignified person. In sharp contrast to the way most trans people are depicted on-screen, Desrae was a very positive role model. That was what made me want to do the series, as well as the fact that I had just joined the cast of *The Good Wife* and had spent the previous few months in a suit playing an uptight politico named Eli Gold. Desrae seemed a nice contrast. I traded the suit for stilettos, happily.

Eli was, and continues to be, quite a revelatory influence in my life, though. He is the first character I have played over a period of years, for starters. Initially I had been reticent about going into a long-running show. I had always done films or theatre, and the little TV I had done was either for a guest spot or for a short season so I always knew what the end of the story was. And now here I was in a situation where my character could suddenly be given a new job, family member or interest with the advent of the next script. It freaked me out a little at first, but now I have come to enjoy the unknown, partly because I have become more comfortable with the concept, and mostly because the writing on the show is so good so I relish any new developments in Eli's world.

It's also exciting when you make a suggestion about your character and very shortly you find yourself acting it out. In the third season I told the show's creators, Robert and Michelle King, that I found it very difficult to imagine being someone who never had sex. There were even mentions in the script by Eli about his lack of action in the bedroom. Lo and behold, mere weeks later I was doing a postcoital scene with the hilarious Amy Sedaris.

When I was offered *The Runaway,* I had only done a few episodes as Eli, but already he was effecting some big changes in me. First of all regarding my hair. As detailed in the first chapter of this book, I have had some issues to overcome in the follicle department, and successfully reclaiming control of my tresses has been achieved via a constantly revolving and eclectic range of haircuts throughout my adulthood. All that was about to stop. Since 2010 I have basically had the same do. I can't actually believe it. It gets a little more edgy in the summer hiatus, the sides a little more clipped perhaps, but nothing really radical since I will be back in that suit by summer's end. Also, and much more significant, it is now *grey!!*

When I started on the show, it was only for one episode and I was shooting during a break from the movie *Burlesque*. My hair had been dyed black for *Burlesque,* and indeed it was coloured regularly for various different projects and often touched up by my hairstylist to keep those pesky grey roots at bay. On the first day of shooting on *The Good Wife*, I spent a long time in the make-up chair having strands of my locks laboriously streaked with grey to give me a more distinguished and, yes, older countenance. After a few episodes, and when I knew I was going to return as a series regular, I told the hairstylist that we could really cut out the middleman. I would just let the colour grow out and embrace my natural salt-and-pepper state. And so I did. Going grey is very interesting because it changes people's attitudes towards you much more than if you'd gone blond or ginger. In some way it means you are embracing middle age or accepting your mortality and owning it. Suddenly I was being called "daddy", and included in fawning magazine articles with other noted salt-and-pepper-locked men. In some way it was assumed I was doing it as a political gesture, embracing my middle age as well as my inner child and trouncing the notion that grey couldn't be sexy. Actually I was not meaning to do any of those things, I just didn't want to have to get up half an hour earlier every day and be poked with grey mascara brushes.

It's also interesting to note that each summer during the hiatus of *The Good Wife,* I have rushed from the relative calm of our studios in Brooklyn to start work on projects that could not be more different in tone or content from Eli's trajectory as a political wheeler and dealer in contemporary Chicago: year one to South Africa to be Desrae; year two to L.A. to shoot *Any Day Now,* in which I play a 1970s drag queen who with his attorney boyfriend attempts to adopt a child with Down syndrome; year three to Scotland to play a man who is admitted to a psychiatric unit and then proceeds to act out the entire play of *Macbeth;* year four mercifully still in New York City, but remounting the crazy that is *Macbeth* on Broadway.

I guess I am not quite at peace with playing middle-aged guys in suits!

As soon as I landed I was plunged back into my life in Cape Town. I was picked up at the airport by my driver, Hodges, a huge African man whose laugh was so bassy and reverberating that the entire car shook when I said something that set him off. It reminded me of my old habit of standing up against a speaker in a club to *feel* the beat. When Hodges laughed, I really felt it. I went straight to the set for a make-up test, then a wardrobe fitting, then back home to the downtown apartment building where most of the cast were barracked, where a lovely manicurist (or nail technician as she preferred to be called) was waiting to reattach the acrylic nails that Desrae sported and I had relinquished before I left for Cannes.

Another thing I relinquished was my body hair. Desrae would not have entertained a hairy arm, and therefore neither did I. Before the first day of filming this series, I had spent an evening in the company of a product called Veet, which, though well known to the female species by other names such as Nair, had hardly ever entered my mental periphery. It is now, however, forever seared into my brain. Do you know what Veet/Nair does? It *dissolves* the hair off your body. Surely this was an invention of the Nazis? You rub it on, sometimes to very sensitive parts of your anatomy, and very soon the hair just *dissolves*. It is not a pretty procedure, and it sure as hell doesn't smell pretty either. But because of Desrae, Veet became a part of my toilette, and I would have to have another application this evening as the stubble on my arms was becoming noticeable. When my *Who Do You Think You Are?* episode was eventually broadcast I was really shocked to see my plucked chicken appearance due to the lack of body hair. It's not a good look for me, believe me.

Playing Desrae made me think of women in a completely different way, and certainly to have a whole new level of respect for them. Aside from the obvious things like the pain of wearing those shoes, I encountered a whole range of new experiences, most of them utterly unpleasant. Bras are not comfortable, for one thing. They are itchy and restricting and have weird wires and springs, making you feel as if you are wearing some sort of cantilever system rather than an article of clothing, which of course you are. Also, I was wearing silicone breasts, or chicken cutlets as they are also known and closely resemble. Silicone crammed against your skin by a bra was a double discomfort whammy, and it was a whole new experience for me to get undressed and find I had a sweaty chest. And dresses and skirts generally don't allow you to open your legs very far. Guys, have you tried getting out of a car without opening your legs recently? You have to sort of scooch along the seat, one buttock at a time, then try and push yourself up on your spindly high heels and hope that you're on a smooth surface when you make contact with the ground.

And nails are another issue. When they're long they clank and catch on things, and even the nail polish made me feel like my nails couldn't breathe. You should have seen the anaemic, soft mess that was left underneath when my acrylic nails were eventually removed (by soaking my fingers in some form of carcinogenic chemical mixture, of course).

Yes, wearing high heels makes your legs look better and your bum look amazing, but I still couldn't help but worry that they were making me more vulnerable at the same time. My bum and my boobs were not just more prominently displayed; it was almost as though the only way I could balance at all was to thrust them out to the world. And what if I wanted to run? Forget about it. If I could have manoeuvred even a light trot in my heels before plunging to the deck, the pain of trying to run in such unnatural and uncomfortable footwear would have laid me up for weeks.

For yes, being a woman, even one with a penis and for the purposes of drama, really made me feel that women have been coerced into a way of presenting themselves that is basically a form of bondage. Their shoes, their skirts, even their nails seem designed to stop them from being able to escape whilst at the same time drawing attention to their sexual and secondary sexual characteristics.

And I think that has happened so that men feel they can ogle them and protect them in equal measure.

Just saying. I was feeling especially vulnerable, for a multitude of reasons, you see.

That night I went to bed duly plucked. Tomorrow I would be up at the crack of dawn and back to work. Tommy Darling's odyssey to Malaysia and the mystery of the final months of his life would remain a mystery for the next month, and the question of whether or not Alex Cumming was my birth father would not be answered for a few days either. I carefully pulled up the blankets with my reattached talons and fell into a deep and grateful sleep.

THEN

I woke up happy in my brother's spare room, and then suddenly remembered what I had to do that day—the scariest thing I would ever do in my life.

I could hear Tom making breakfast downstairs.

The night before we had talked it all through and I had written it all down in case I got so nervous that I couldn't remember anything. I was really worried I wasn't going to be able to get through it. As soon as I had started to have the flashbacks, I knew in my heart that the only way I was going to be able to get better, to truly exorcise the pain and move on, was to one day talk to my father about it all.

They had started in my dreams, dark dispatches dropped into my sleep that I began to realise were nightmares that had actually happened. Soon after, I didn't need to be asleep. My stomach would knot up and I could see my father's face coiled in rage as though it was yesterday. I could hear the dull ringing in my ears that was left after he made contact with my head. The sting, the dizziness, the inability to breathe, the humiliation, the shame, the despair that had been recorded in my mind so many years before now played back for the first time.

I had cut myself off from my life. I was now in a cocoon with no responsibilities of work or marriage. I left the little flat mostly to eat or to go to therapy. The rest of the time I was free to just feel, to remember, and mourn. I realised I had never just *stopped* like this in my entire life. Finally now I was ready to go where I needed to go. What started as a trickle soon turned into a flood. I spent days just gazing at the ceiling of my little flat, remembering and reliving pieces of my childhood that I could now fully access. It was truly horrifying, but it was also incredibly liberating because in accessing these horrible memories I was beginning to understand who I really was. Such a huge part of my psyche had been closed off for so long, and now I was embracing the fullness of my life experience for the first time.

It's hard to express how fragile I felt in those early days. To begin with, I was terrified to tell anyone what I was experiencing. Partly because the memories were so raw and painful that it was difficult to talk about it at all without collapsing, and partly because I had a great fear of not being believed. And then I felt anxious about the prospect of talking about all of this with Tom and Mum. What if they weren't ready and I was forcing them to confront a morass of pain and shame that they never wanted to revisit? Worse, what if they couldn't deal with it at all? What if they didn't believe me?

I needn't have worried. I talked to Mum first. My domestic situation had obviously changed and she was naturally worried about why. We spoke on the phone one night and I told her what had been happening, how I had begun to remember so many awful things that Dad had done and was now beginning to understand the vastness of how much I had been damaged by him. She couldn't have been more loving and understanding. She told me she'd always worried that this part of my past was going to come back and haunt me. We spoke as two survivors, now finally able to acknowledge our shared past.

A couple of days later I saw Tom, and over a long dinner we talked quite calmly and precisely about many, many instances of our father's madness and violence. It was good to do so in such a rational, unemotional way. It made it all real and valid. We walked through the streets of London deep in conversation, both of us feeding each other forgotten nuggets of memory. We expressed to each other for the first time how we had felt in many, many instances of shame and violence we had endured. When we arrived at where Tom was staying, we hugged goodnight and suddenly we both began weeping uncontrollably, our chests heaving with grief for the two little scared boys we had been for so long.

All that summer *sorting myself out* in Primrose Hill I had been working up to this day. I'd been seeing a therapist for many months, and early on he had told me that a confrontation would be a necessary part of my recovery. Even Mary Darling had said I should. Tom and I both agreed that we needed to do it, but it was easier said than done. We were effectively going back to the place where it had all happened to confront our abuser about incidents and memories that had just recently appeared back in our psyches and were still incredibly raw and painful.

But we were now ready, I hoped. I picked up the papers from the bedside table and read over what I had written. It seemed so weird to see the entire thing encapsulated so neatly. Only two pages of A4, but packed with portent:

Dad

The way you behaved towards us throughout our childhood has had a huge effect on us, and has caused us many problems. You brutalised and terrorised us. We were made to feel useless, unworthy; we lived in constant fear of you. Not just of being hit but also of being constantly shouted at and brought down and tormented.

We were never good enough for you. We could never live up to your expectations. We were made to feel we were not capable of doing anything. You would ask us to do tasks for you that we couldn't possibly achieve, and then you would chastise us and hit us for not doing them well enough. So consequently we've gone through life feeling unhappy and unable to acknowledge our achievements because we still feel unworthy—as being told we are useless is so ingrained in us.

We have made excuses for your behaviour all our lives. We were embarrassed because people laughed and didn't believe us if we told them about the violence, about you stopping us from going to things at the last minute, the way you made us work all the time, and so we started to make up excuses for you, so much so that we all pretended that nothing was really wrong and none of this ever happened, until it exploded out earlier this summer.

But we also felt it was our fault. We were led to believe that the reason you hit us, the reason you went out nearly every night, the reason you had very obvious affairs, the reason Mum was unhappy was all our fault. Because you told us we were useless, and we believed you and took all the blame for ourselves.

But we are not useless.

As children, when we most needed support and

encouragement and love, when we were at our most vulnerable and impressionable, we had as a role model a man who hit us and never encouraged us or said a positive thing to us. We felt unloved. You didn't really like us. Maybe you still don't.

You had a problem with violence. We would have been taken into the care of the authorities if they had found out about the extent and regularity of your violence. Hitting an eight-year-old boy so hard that he is thrown across a room is not right. You would have been arrested on many occasions. You had no control over your temper. You totally flipped. You had psychopathic tendencies. We lived in constant fear. We were terrified of our own father, the man who should have been protecting us.

You never encouraged us to pursue our own interests so we consequently had to keep them secret. You would stop us from leaving the house to go out. We felt no security in our own decisions and skills.

We want to say all this to you to make you understand how we feel, and how we have been affected by the past. And that not having spoken about it is so wrong and damaging for everyone.

We want you to somehow acknowledge that you remember some of the things we are talking about.

In some way talking about it is acknowledging that it happened. And we are releasing the past, letting it go so we can all move forward and on.

We are giving you back the things you gave us.

I put the papers down. So many thoughts were whirring through my head. Tom and I had both been through a summer of intense examination and analysis of the events of the past, but I was nervous that suddenly springing all this on our father would alienate him and do the exact opposite of what we both intended and needed, which was some sort of acknowledgement of his actions and ownership of the past. I didn't want to scare him away, but I wanted him to hear the truth too.

But also, I had no choice in the matter. I *had* to do this. I knew it. Tom knew it. Our whole lives had been leading up to this moment. We were going to give back to our father that which was not ours, and what we never should have been given in the first place.

Tom had called him earlier in the week to ask if we could come and see him as we needed to talk about some things, so my father must have grasped that this was not merely a pleasant family trip. The very fact that we were visiting at all was a rarity by this point. I hadn't seen him for several years. Since I'd moved to London in 1988, the visits out of duty had grown more and more sporadic. When I was married, and my wife and I regularly came to stay with my in-laws who lived a few miles away, I often didn't even let my father know I was coming. And he certainly never visited me. In fact, I realised in the run-up to this monumental meeting that my father had never once called me on the telephone in my entire adult life. He had spoken to me, sure, after the phone was passed to him by my mother, and once my parents separated, I had called him, but he had never once picked up the phone himself and dialled my number.

I had flown up to Scotland from London the night before, and spent the evening talking and remembering with Tom. We both knew how right this was, how necessary, but it still scared the shit out of us. We'd had a good few drinks to lighten our spirits and gird our loins, and now, here we were, the next day, in his car on our way to Panmure, about to confront our father with our childhood demons.

As we passed through the gates and the big looming sign that read PRIVATE: AUTHORISED PERSONS ONLY my heart began to pound. Everything seemed to be floating by in slow motion. The head gamekeeper's house, the cottages where the wife of one of my father's workers had taught me piano, the little box at the corner that I'd rush to every Saturday morning to collect my comic book. By the time we turned right and could see the sawmill yard, my hands had begun to shake.

"I'm not sure I can do this, Tom," I said, my breath suddenly shallow, my mouth so dry I could barely swallow. And I was totally serious. I felt completely out of my depth, like the little boy I once was walking down this road into a world that made no sense and that was so out of my control.

"You're going to be fine. I'm here with you. We're doing this together," said Tom.

We pulled up in front of the house and sat for a moment in

the car just staring at the grey stone edifice before us. Sometimes when you come back to places from your childhood they seem smaller, less daunting. But this place seemed as bleak and gothic and unwelcoming as it had when we were little boys.

"You okay?" Tom asked.

"I think so," I whispered.

"Just try and stay calm and not let him get to you."

"I'm really scared," I said.

"Remember, he doesn't control us any more, Alan."

I loved my brother so much in that moment.

We got out of the car and rang the doorbell, but then moved back up the drive a bit, as though to protect ourselves from a looming explosion. After a moment our father appeared through the mottled glass of the porch, like a memory coming back into focus. We watched him, hanging back, gauging him. Then he opened the door.

"Aye," he said. "Are you coming in?"

Tom and I had both decided that we couldn't enter the house. It would be too unnerving to discuss past incidents that may have occurred in the very room we were sitting in. And also we didn't want to do this in his territory, be trapped on his home turf.

"We'd actually like to go for a walk, if that's okay with you," said Tom.

"Oh aye," he murmured and disappeared into the house, returning moments later in a jacket, and with a large rough-hewn wooden stick in his hand. His little West Highland Terrier scampered up to us, breaking the tension that was beginning to crackle all around.

"You're wanting to talk about something," he began, hitting his stick against the side of his work boot as we began to walk up the yard.

"Yes, we are." I was amazed to hear my voice, quite calm, quite strong. "We want to talk to you about stuff that happened when we were little."

He said nothing, but cleared his throat noisily and spat into a drain.

Undaunted, I continued. "I don't know if you know, but I've been having a bit of a bad time recently."

"I hear your marriage has broken up," he said suddenly and accusingly.

"That's right," I said, trying not to let him needle me. "It has." I put my hand in my pocket to feel the bits of paper for reassurance.

"I've been in a bit of a state for most of this year actually. And my marriage fell apart under the strain of . . . of . . . of that." I was beginning to stumble. This wasn't good.

"Is it definitely over?" he asked. What was this, concern? No, surely not. That was never in his lexicon. Could it possibly be he was using the failure of my marriage as a smokescreen for what he'd somehow intuited was going to be a condemnation of him? Was he trying to shift the focus? That made sense. He was like an animal now, sizing me up, sniffing my fear.

"Eh, yes." I felt the weight of my words, their portent, their resignation. "Yes, it's definitely over. We're getting a divorce," I said, careful to cede no weakness with this statement. I had jumped off the cliff now. This was on. Tom glanced over at me, willing me strength.

"Part of the reason that happened is that I had a bit of a breakdown earlier in the year and it made it harder and harder for me to be able to function. And I remembered a lot of things that both Tom and I had suppressed for many, many years. Memories of things that had happened in our childhood, things you did that we don't think were right . . . and we've come today to talk to you about them."

"Oh aye," he said again, and began walking up the yard away from us, whistling for his dog as he did so.

The walk was a very long one. We went all the way down to the other end of the estate, nearly to the Garden House where as a young boy I'd gone to pick the raspberries that now adorned its once ornate terraces. At this point, my dad turned on Tom, goading him about how often he saw his eldest son, from his previous marriage. It was as though our father really was trying to equate his actions with our failed relationships, and perhaps he had a point, though not the one I am sure he intended. A successful relationship requires a level of self-knowledge and comfort with oneself, and neither Tom nor I had much of that at the moment. We were stumbling towards it, but only just. These past few months had completely changed us both. We had spent so many nights on the phone, relaying to each other a new memory, backing up dim visions with the assurance that the other had the same memory. That what we remembered was real.

It is a startling thing, the need to feel utterly believed. Memories that were so tender and tentative could not be entrusted to anyone who might possibly doubt them during those months I was sequestered in Primrose Hill, *sorting myself out.* Tom and I were only just beginning to believe and fully understand the scope of what we'd been through, so it was so important to us to hear that we were accepted and understood.

Luckily we had waited until our arsenal of memories was so vivid that our father's most intense scare tactics and mind games could not shake us. But believe me, he tried his hardest. Nobody plays nice when he is cornered, but for a man like him it was the most uncomfortable and painful place to be, and he was not equipped for it, aside from falling back on his default behaviours of manipulation and intimidation.

My most vivid memory of our conversation is of my father's utter silence. I had said that I knew he must remember some of what we were speaking of, and his silence, aside from a whistle for the dog and the vicious thump to the inside of his boot with his stick, was proof that he did.

"What was your childhood like?" I asked him. "Did Granddad hit you?" I was both fascinated and scared about the prospect of my father not being able to break a circle of abuse because that might mean I would be unable to too. He ignored me.

"Did you never feel bad about hitting us?" Again he started off in front of us, desperate to avoid. But we were in the middle of the estate's most huge and sprawling drive. There were no cars coming, there was nobody around. There was nowhere to run. I scampered after him.

"D'you think you hit us because you were so unhappy in your marriage?"

He turned to me, fury in his eyes.

"My marriage was over four years after Tommy was born," he spat.

I stopped in my tracks, shocked, and watched him as he walked away.

"Thanks," I called after him. "That's two years before I was even born. That makes me feel great."

Tom was beside me, his hand on the small of my back, propelling me down the drive to catch up with him.

"Why didn't you leave then?" I demanded when we had caught up with him.

"I had kids to think of," he replied with a mixture of indignation and righteousness that was both galling and horribly predictable. Of course he would be able to justify his presence in our lives, the very presence that allowed his sons to be repeatedly abused, with his fatherly duty to protect them.

"I had kids to think of," he actually said, staring at the very kids who were then doing their best to explain to this man that he had never once thought of their welfare. That his care of them had not been care at all.

"Where were they?" I said to his retreating back. "Where were these kids you were thinking of? Cos they sure as hell weren't Tom and me."

His only response was the usual litany of spitting, banging his boot with his stick, and whistling for the dog.

Finally we were back at the house and wrapping things up. We had said everything we had wanted to. We had countered every trick and bullying technique he had tried to pull with solidarity and strength. I had thought he was actually going to hit me once, when I'd said that if he thought that his abusive behaviour was not connected to unhappiness or events in his own life, then he was basically admitting that he was psychotic. It was a big word, I knew. But seriously. Again his stick had banged against his boot several times, and eventually he turned his gaze towards me and stared deep into my eyes. I knew what he wanted to do. I had seen that look many, many times before. But what would happen now if he tried it? I would most certainly retaliate. Tom would come to my aid. During this stare-off I visualised my father on the ground, restrained and spitting like the angry, bewildered animal he was.

But he backed down. "I am not a psychopath," he seethed and marched ahead once more.

"Thank you," I said, and I truly meant it. "Thank you for letting us come here today and get this off our chests. I hope you understand how much we needed to do this. And I hope you understand that we want to move on and put this behind us, and if you want to have a relationship with us, we are willing to have one with you. But you'll need to make an effort; you have to reach out. You need to show us that you care about continuing. We are not coming to see you out of duty any more. This has to be a two-way thing. So the ball's in your court."

We got back in the car, and as soon as we were out of sight of the house we both burst into screams of joy and relief. I couldn't believe we had done it! Not just done it. We had triumphed! We had spoken honestly and without malice, we had stood up to him, we had truly given back to him that which was not ours and which we should never have had to deal with in the first place.

"You did great, Alan!" Tom smiled at me. "And you hardly looked at the script at all!"

As we were getting into the car, our father had started to back away from us and turned quickly towards the house. As he did so I could see there were tears in his eyes. I could tell we had truly connected with him. Maybe there was hope that he would step up to the plate after all.

I never heard from him again.

FRIDAY 4TH JUNE 2010

I t's amazing how quickly your life can return to normal. Well, that is if your normal is getting up at 5 A.M. and spending a couple of hours transforming yourself into a lady and then pretending said lovely lady is in various states of distress, mourning, or sexual compromise.

With each day that passed, I filled my head a little more with my work and my colleagues, and every day brought a new scene, new actors, often a new decade. And of course new costumes. Desrae was not a twin-set-and-pearls kind of gal. Even off duty from the club, and doing a spot of light shopping with her adopted daughter, she dressed to the nines. The runaway, Cathy, was played by Joanna Vanderham, a fellow Scot I nicknamed "Perth" because of her birthplace, and with whom I spent many a morning chortling away at the latest ensemble I had donned.

Cape Town was also in a state of frenzy about the looming World Cup. The whole city felt like it was in one of those home improvement TV shows where someone is tricked into going away for a couple of days and in their absence loads of people descend on their house and garden and remodel them in a flash. Each morning on the way to work I would see new trees along the side of the road that had been planted in the night, pavements being repaved, the entire population united in giving their city a sparkly makeover to counter the glare of the world's attention. It was an exciting time to be there, to be sure, but also an anxious one. Just like on those TV shows, I worried that they wouldn't be finished in time, and all the work would be for naught. But of course, just like on those TV shows, they pulled it out of the bag, and the world descended and was in awe at this gleaming metropolis, little knowing that the paint was barely dry.

Then of course the tournament started and the makeover frenzy turned to the competition. The South Africans called their team "Bafana Bafana", which means "boys boys". I loved that. Imagine how much more affectionate it would feel if Scotland, sadly a non-qualifier for this World Cup, called its national team "lads lads" or "fellas fellas"!

Sometimes, when we were working during a match, our filming would have to be halted due to the sheer volume of the locals' cheering when Bafana Bafana scored. Sometimes we had to stop because the cheering came from some of our crew! And then of course there were the *vuvuzellas,* plastic horns that became a constant soundscape during my time in Cape Town. At first I found them fun and spirited. I myself am no stranger to a good loud whistle or kazoo at certain times of celebration. But the sheer volume, and the sheer *volume* of the *vuvuzellas* made them soon lose their original appeal and eventually become almost maddening. If you saw some of the games on television and despaired at their constant cacophony, just imagine living in a city where that sound was a constant 24/7. After a while I perfected a way to zone them out, but I was only able to do so when they were played en masse. A lone *vuvuzella* being blown in the car park beneath my apartment in the middle of the night was enough to send me spiralling into nail-scratching irritation.

It was a heady time to be in South Africa, though, so much so that when I returned to my trailer on the Friday of my first week back to find an e-mail from my office with the subject "DNA test results", I was jolted back into a world I had almost forgotten existed. I was ashamed at how quickly I had moved on.

THEN

Once, a long time ago, when I was a very little boy and before the troubles started, my father went into the hospital for an operation. I know it was a long time ago and before it all went bad because I remember that on the day he was to return home I ran as fast as my little legs could carry me when the school bus dropped me off at the gates in order to get home and see him. I had missed him, you see.

When I got there, breathless, he was nowhere to be seen. I looked in the living room, the kitchen, his office, even the Good Room that nobody ever went into except at Christmas. Where could he be? I went upstairs to my parents' bedroom to see if he was there, but no.

Finally I wondered if he hadn't been released from hospital after all, but made one last-ditch attempt and opened the door to the spare bedroom downstairs. That's another reason why I know it was a long time ago before it all went bad—that bedroom became my mum's shortly afterwards, but then it was still the spare.

I opened the door quickly and rushed in, not expecting to see anything, let alone the horror I encountered. My father was asleep on his back, his face a mess of bruises and bloody bandages. He looked like Frankenstein's monster. I was terrified.

He didn't stir, thankfully, and I immediately turned on my heels and left the room, pulled the door carefully shut, and walked away through to the kitchen to set the table and do my chores.

I decided it hadn't happened. I hadn't seen him.

When my mum came home, she asked me if I'd seen my father and I lied and said no. We went through together to the spare room and woke him up. He still scared me, but the shock of seeing him had been diminished. I pretended to be more shocked than I actually was. I acted, maybe properly for the first time. My parents comforted me.

For the first time in my childhood, but certainly not the last, I encountered an upsetting experience and decided the best way to deal with it was to pretend it had never happened. And so it didn't.

Here's what did happen: my father's broken nose was straightened and his breathing and sinus problems were over, and during his recovery period he was tended to by a nurse whom he began an affair with, and all our lives were changed forever.

FRIDAY 4TH JUNE 2010

My hand was trembling as I clicked open the e-mail. There was an attachment with the actual medical report, and for a few moments I couldn't see anything but a blur of letters and numbers. Eventually I saw that on the left there was a list of the various components of the overall test and then two columns on the right that showed my results and Tom's. At the end of every single line the numbers were the same. I looked down the list. The same series of figures. Every one.

I was gasping. Perhaps the fact that I had so willingly immersed myself in my imaginary life here in South Africa made the shock even more pronounced. I kept staring at the lists and columns in front of me, and eventually they began to vibrate and go out of focus. I sat up and walked in a circle and immediately sat down again. I e-mailed my assistant.

Brian, I'm in a state. I want to be really sure. Just confirm to me that this means Tom and I have the same father. Thanks. Alan

I got up and began changing out of Desrae's costume. There was a knock on the door and a wardrobe assistant came in to collect my clothes. I handed them to her in a daze and wished her a good night. Then I heard the familiar *ping* of an incoming e-mail on my computer. I leapt back into the chair and opened it.

Yes, your DNA and Tom's DNA absolutely match. He is your father. I'm so sorry.

Immediately rage overwhelmed me. I opened my mouth and let out a roar so deep and primal and furious that I scared myself. My knees buckled and I flopped down into the chair again.

THEN

I'd rushed home from work every night for weeks hoping that the letter would have come, but each night I was disappointed.

I had a job now, and so my father had less sway over me. I didn't have to work on the estate any more, except during times when extra hands were really needed, like the previous Christmas when I'd worked weekends and evenings selling trees. People would ring our bell and I'd walk them to the tractor shed where, on pulling open the doors, a blast of intense pine from the hundreds of felled spruce trees piled high against the walls assaulted your nose.

I used to hate Christmas because it would mean working late into the dark, freezing night cutting trees, carting them to the sawmill yard, pushing their prickly, sappy carcasses through a tube to encase them in nylon netting, and carrying them to the buyers' cars or piling them high onto carts to be transported to shops in local towns. I also had to fake civility with my father in these cases. He was careful to appear strict but fair whenever we were in groups of people like this, careful to vent his habitual ire in the safety of the house or in the dark corner of a shed.

Now, though, he had to *ask* me for my help, not order me. I was seventeen. I was a man. I was working as a sub-editor in a publishing house in Dundee and I paid for my own keep. Each morning I cycled past my father up the sawmill yard, still mindful of his disapproving eye. In my rucksack I would have my preferred clothes (tight red jeans, black suede Tukka boots, and a jacket with pins of my favourite bands' logos on the lapels), and after I'd left the estate premises, his fiefdom, I'd change into them behind a tree and make my way down the hill to the village of Barry, feeling liberated and edgy, where I'd be picked up by a work colleague and driven to the big city of Dundee.

I'd auditioned for drama school late in the spring. Mum had gone to Glasgow with me and was waiting on the steps as I came running out to tell her I'd been called back for the second round of improvisation later that afternoon. We went for lunch, but I could barely eat, I was so excited. Then, at the end of the day, we got the train back home and I daydreamed about the life that seemed tantalisingly within my grasp.

I had no idea you could actually go to university and study to be an actor. I hadn't even really entertained the possibility that it could ever be anything other than a hobby for me. Then I heard that a girl a couple of years above me at secondary school had gone to somewhere called the "Academy". It sounded so impossibly grand and out of my realm, but the more I researched, the more I knew it was where I wanted to go, where I needed to go. It was my salvation.

My parents were initially very wary of the idea, but the fact that I'd get a degree at the end of it reassured them. The phrase "something to fall back on" was oft repeated around that time. I wasn't sure exactly what it was I would be falling back from or on, but I didn't care. I just wanted out.

"There's a letter for you," my mum said, thrusting the envelope into my hand as I came in the door still sweaty from the bike ride up the Marches hill. The postmark was Glasgow. It was typed, not handwritten. I flipped it over, the return address confirming that this was indeed the letter I'd been waiting for.

"I'll leave you to open it on your own," and she was gone into the kitchen.

My hands trembled. The next few seconds would either change my life or . . . what? I hadn't auditioned for or applied to any other schools. I was still too young to be considered for university. I would have to wait another whole year before I'd have a chance like this again.

"I got in!" I yelled in joy, and immediately the kitchen door flew open and Mum rushed in to hug me.

"I start in September!" I said in disbelief. I was going to be free.

"I'm so proud of you, son." She turned away from me, sobs gurgling up from somewhere deep. I went upstairs to the Big Room and sat staring out at the fields and fields of green. I was numb. It was actually going to happen.

When I went down again to eat, my father was home. Mum had obviously told him my news.

"Aye. That's the response you were looking for, was it?" he said, as he passed me on the way to the kitchen.

"Yes," I replied to his back.

FRIDAY 4TH JUNE 2010, SECONDS LATER

I remembered that Tom was copied on the e-mail too, and I picked up my phone to call him, but I knew that I couldn't have that conversation here. I needed to be alone and at home, so I tried to calm myself down enough to be able to walk to Hodges' car and get back to my apartment.

I picked up my bags and opened the trailer door. I said friendly good-byes to crew members I passed, signed my name on the union time sheet, took my call sheet for the next day's filming, and then I was off.

You know how sometimes you don't intend to do something and then you do and it turns out to be the best thing you ever could have done?

I told Hodges.

"I have to phone my father tonight and tell him that I am actually his son, Hodges," I blurted.

The old man's eyes widened, but he kept his eyes on the road.

"I think you need to start at the beginning, Alan," he said calmly.

I told him everything. He already knew all about *Who Do You Think You Are?* and Tommy Darling, as he had shared my excitement in the lead-up to the start of filming and was anxious to hear the revelations on my return. But I hadn't told him about my father. He listened in silence as I unravelled before him. It seemed even more surreal and ridiculous when I heard it spoken out loud. We had arrived at the apartment building and I was still going, so Hodges turned off the ignition and waited patiently for me to finish.

"So now I'm going upstairs and I'm going to speak to my brother and then I'm going to call my father and tell him," I said finally.

"You must not do that, Alan!" he said quietly but firmly.

I was startled into silence. I looked across at his unblinking eyes trained on me. He was sad for me, which was clear. But he looked serious too. He meant what he had said.

"You are angry. You have a right to be angry, and you should be angry, but you must not call your father in anger. Speak to your brother, get it out of your system with him, and then sleep. Call your father tomorrow when anger will not cloud what you need to say to him."

I opened my mouth to speak but nothing came out. He was right of course.

"Thank you, Hodges," I managed eventually.

"You are welcome, Alan. Sleep well."

Wisdom and guidance can come from the most unexpected places.

Tom had the same reaction as me: rage. We spoke for a long time, going round and round in circles trying to make sense of it all. Why had he done this? Was it the last hurrah of a heartless dying man? Did he really set out to confuse and upset us one last time? Surely not. Surely not even he was capable of such cruelty.

But if not that, then why? Had he truly believed this? Had he harboured this suspicion all my life and only now, when he thought it might come out publicly, had he felt forced to reveal it?

That didn't make sense either. We talked about our early childhood, before his affairs and our beatings had become so regular and prevalent. If he had believed this from my birth, why would he have waited so many years to enact his warped revenge? Was he seriously waiting for me to grow old enough that he could start beating me? What about the way he treated Tom? He was his undoubted heir, and he beat him just the same.

The only sense we could make of it was that yet again we were his victims. After all these years he was still able to surprise us with the depths of his . . . what? Cruelty? Cowardice? Check. Madness?

I had always thought my father was an angry, violent man, frustrated and trapped like an animal in a cage, lashing out at those weaker than himself to blame them for, and validate, his situation. But now I was beginning to think there might be more to it than mere venom. I started to consider the possibility that my father was simply mentally ill.

But I realised I couldn't go down that particular rabbit hole right now. There was something more pressing and more important to think about: Mum. We would have to tell her this story, and I knew it would devastate her. Not just by the enormity of the lie that my father believed to be true, but by the longevity of its effects on us all.

I said good-night to Tom. We were both exhausted, but the chat had done us good. It was exactly two weeks since that night in London when Tom had come round and we had gone onto the roof deck. Two weeks in which I had clung eagerly to the belief that I was not my father's son. Now all that was dashed. Now I had to readjust to the fact, the absolute medical fact, that I was. Of course it was good to know the truth, but it was hard to let go of the fantasy I had carried and nurtured for the past fourteen days.

"You know, I was so happy not to be his son," I said, as Tom and I were hanging up.

"But at least now I know I'm your full brother."

SATURDAY 5TH JUNE 2010

As soon as the first assistant director called lunch, my stomach clenched. I went back to my trailer and ate the food that was waiting for me. I had never chewed my food so well.

I reached for my phone, and dialled his number.

"Hello," he said. The signal was scratchy and weak.

"It's Alan," I began.

"Oh yes."

"I'm calling to tell you I got the results of the DNA test and I want you to know that I *am* your son."

Almost immediately he replied, "Well I'm very glad to hear that."

Then the line went dead.

I leapt back in my seat. What? What had he just said? He was *glad*?! And did he hang up on me? He couldn't have. It must be the connection. I rang again. The line was slightly better this time.

"Yes?"

"I don't think you heard me properly," I began again. "I got the results and I *am* your son." I had never enunciated so clearly.

There was silence at the other end of the line. I wondered if I'd lost him again.

"Well, I'm very surprised to hear that," he said, sounding genuinely shocked.

"I bet you are," I replied.

I waited for him to make the next move. I could feel his mind whirring, trying to make sense of it all. The tables had turned, for once.

"Are you absolutely sure?" he asked.

"Totally. I can send you a copy of the results if you like. Tom and I have identical Y chromosomes. Believe me, if I wasn't your son I would not lie to you about it."

I checked myself. I was getting mean. My anger was seeping through. I needed to not alienate him. This was my last ever chance to try and understand him and why he had done this, and I mustn't blow it.

"It never happened, Dad. You imagined it all. Mum never had an affair. None of it ever happened."

"But I had to believe it, Alan . . . ," he said incredulously (and incredibly).

This really intrigued me. "You *had* to?" I replied. "Why?"

"I saw them coming out of the room . . ."

"Whatever you saw was innocent. You made it all up." I felt like I was talking to a child, or someone coming round from an anaesthetic and needing to have everything reiterated again and again.

"I saw what I saw," he said, over and over.

"No," I countered. "You saw what you wanted to see, or what you decided you'd seen."

There was silence. I could feel him regrouping and preparing for his next salvo.

"But you must have known . . . ," he began.

I tried to imagine how much of a shock this must be for him, but I was the one who was shocked about his inability to accept the truth, let alone to consider what I, and Tom, had been through these last two weeks. It was utterly illuminating and predictable at the same time.

"How could I have known, Dad? It never happened. You imagined it. It was a figment of your imagination. I am your son."

I wondered if I should just hang up. He was obviously not capable of dealing with this information, or reality in any form. Perhaps I should give him some time to process everything. I could call back in a day or two. But then I thought, *What would be the point of that?* I had more important things to contend with, like talking to Mum, and taking care of myself. That was when he blindsided me.

"I didn't do this to hurt you, Alan."

I inhaled in the way you do when you're about to cry. It felt like an apology, although technically it wasn't, but it was enough to stop me in my tracks to marvel at how it felt to hear my father show some feeling, some tenderness. But was that truly what he was doing? His first line of defence had failed—perhaps now he was trying to emotionally manipulate me.

I realised how tired I was of trying to second-guess him. I'd been doing it for over forty years. "Look, I believe that you believed this. I don't think that you just made it up. But you have hurt me. You have hurt me all my life. And you've hurt Tom and you've hurt Mum," I said calmly.

"But you know we never bonded," was my father's response. That was it.

"Maybe we never bonded because you were treating me like shit because you thought I was another man's child," I said.

I could feel him reel.

"There's no need for that," he said, anger in his voice.

"There's every need for it. You have lived your life based on a false assumption. And the fact that you are trying to use that to justify the way you abused me is really despicable."

And in that instant I saw the double blow of his justifying that abuse in any way at all, let alone based on a figment of his imagination.

"I had to believe it," he offered again, scared now and repeating himself.

"No, you didn't, because you made it up. There was nothing to believe."

I almost felt sorry for him, but I wanted to say one last thing, one thing that needed to be said. One thing that I never thought I'd have the strength to say.

"It never happened. And I can't believe you never talked to Mum about it, and you had to wait for me . . ." My voice squeaked a little. I was starting to lose it, but I knew this was nearly over and I had to get it out. "I had to be the one to tell you the truth. For forty-five years you never had the balls to find out the truth for yourself. You just acted upon a suspicion, you based your entire life upon a false assumption and you made all our lives hell."

I waited for a response. Surely, surely he could give me something. Just some acknowledgement that he understood the enormity of the pain he had caused, at least in the last two weeks, if not for a lifetime.

I should have known better.

"I've decided I won't be talking to that *Sunday Mail* fellow," he said, as though what I had said had never happened. He sounded almost breezy. I could tell he thought he was throwing me a bone, giving me something positive. He reminded me of addicts I've known, lighting fires around themselves as a smoke-screen to mask the real issue.

"You know, I really don't care if you speak to them or not," I said and I truly meant it. "I'm going to go now. I imagine you have a lot of processing to do, considering you now have to reassess the past forty-five years."

Silence.

"Okay, take care. I'll talk to you soo—" I stopped. What was I saying? If ever there was a time for the truth it was now.

"Actually, I won't be speaking to you again, but take care."

"Aye," was the last thing my father ever said to me.

"Bye," I said and hung up.

I looked up at myself in the mirror of my trailer. I had just had the most horrible conversation of my life, and the very last conversation I would ever have with my tormentor. I was free of him at last. I wonder what he would have done had he known that during that conversation I was wearing high heels, a bra and panties, and a full face of make-up.

Now of course I had to tell Mary Darling. I knew that eventually I would have to talk to her one way or the other, but this outcome was always going to be the hardest. Had it gone the other way, and I was not my father's son, I would have gone to her with elation, curiosity too of course about the reason she had kept it a secret for so long, but elation both for her and for me. Now I went to her with dread, and knew the only outcome would be upset and anger and sadness. Again.

I even considered not telling her at all. But we had spoken several times over the past two weeks, in reference to her father's unfolding story, about the importance of being open and not having secrets in a family, and how good it ultimately is to know the truth. So how could I consider staying silent?

Over the years, my father had become estranged not just from his wife, his sons and his grandchildren but also most of his other immediate family. If ever there was an example of the dangers of failing to communicate, Alex Cumming was it.

I wrote the whole story down. I knew I couldn't tell her the whole thing over the phone. There was just too much to it and it was still very raw for me. I also knew that on the telephone, I wouldn't be able to hold it together, and my mum would become upset hearing me so devastated. Plus, writing it down made it more real, somehow—this wasn't all a nightmare that I woke from screaming. It had, in fact, happened.

I got it all down in a long and emotional e-mail. Then I called Mary Darling to tell her the message was coming. She wasn't in, and I left her a voice mail.

> "Mum. It's Alan. Ahh, look, I don't know any other way
> to do this. I'm about to send you an e-mail that you'll find
> shocking and upsetting. It's about Dad. Tom and I are fine,
> we're both fine. Don't worry about us. But we've had some

interactions with Dad and it's been awful and I wrote you
an e-mail so you would have all the information, and once
you've read it and you're ready to talk, please call me. I
love you, Mum. Okay? I have to go now. Take care."

There was a huge stone of hurt and sadness in my belly, the
visit of an old acquaintance who needed to leave. I hoped that
this story I had typed out, with tears in my eyes, would close the
door once and for all. I scanned the text all the way down to the
last paragraph . . .

It's amazing how Dad can still, even as he comes to the end of his
life, cause such drama and pain to us all. Tom and I are here for you,
Mum, and love you, and never stopped loving you throughout any
of it.

Alan x

The next day we spoke. She'd had an awful night, sleepless and
anguished. But the first thing she said when she picked up the
phone has stayed with me, and always will.

"I never knew he had so much evil in him, Alan."

Part Two

CANCEL,
CONTINUE.

I had two more weeks filming in Cape Town before I could return to New York, to Grant, and to getting on with my life. Luckily I was busy working every day, and the little spare time I did have was filled with seeing friends who were in town or dinners with the producers and the cast of the mini-series.

I told a couple of people the story. It just came out over a drink, but it was too soon and too weird and too inappropriate to really unleash it all. When I got home to New York I knew I'd have to start the process of normalising this chapter of my life, making it something that had happened to me, not something that I was still living.

I had that empty, nagging ache inside like someone had died, or I'd been attacked. And of course, both things were true. My father was dead to me now, but he'd certainly left his marks on me before I'd shut the door on him. Technically, I suppose he'd shut the door on Tom and me sixteen years ago, that cold November afternoon when he walked back into our childhood home with tears in his eyes. That would probably have been the last time

I'd ever have spoken to him had this not happened. I decided I was actually thankful for the opportunity to have proper closure. Bizarrely, after all these years and all that had happened, it felt like an amicable split. No hard feelings, just gobsmacked amazement. I wished him well. I truly did. And, for perhaps the first time in my life, I felt sorry for him.

Over the next few weeks I spoke to Tom and Mum often. We checked in with each other, gauging where the other was in the grieving process, for that is truly what it was. My mum had dreamt of the outcome of my appearance on *Who Do You Think You Are?* as giving her the answers about her father she had always longed for. Instead, my father had intervened and ruined her chance for pure happiness. Mary Darling had no idea that her husband had harboured such beliefs about her for all those years. In the many talks with her that followed, I began to formulate my initial theories about why and, more importantly, *when* he had begun to believe that I was not his son.

Mum remembered the night in question, all those years ago in Dunkeld at the dance in the hotel. But her version of events was quite different. She had not gone to another room. They had not been discovered. She told me that the man in question, my supposed father, had a bit of a drink problem and she remembered him needing to talk about it that night. So not only was my father gravely mistaken in his impression of what had gone on between them, he had also seen an act of kindness and consideration on my mother's part as betrayal and deceit. Of course that made perfect sense. I remembered how easily my dad could see the negative in any exchange.

More and more, as we dug further into the past, I began to remember how deeply and often my father twisted reality into the paranoia-filled world he inhabited. I relived many occasions in my childhood when his anger erupted illogically. He would suddenly take against someone or something for reasons that were often impossible to fathom, certainly to a little boy, and because usually he would not voice them. As soon as his mind was made up, there could be no mention of the person or thing without risking his rage. Whether we liked it or not, we too had to make that person or thing disappear.

But in the case of my conception, there had been no outbursts or fury. My father's version of the event at the hotel, with him grabbing my mum and saying, "Well there's no point in staying here any longer," did not ring any bells with her at all. It was as shocking for her to hear it as it had been for me.

I asked Mum if she could remember anything at all in his behaviour while she was pregnant with me that hinted at his suspicion. She couldn't.

Indeed she told me a very touching story about my father rushing down the hill to get her fish and chips from the village to quell her pregnancy cravings, and also how happy he had been when I was brought home from the hospital. But with that story of his rare thoughtfulness came another bit of truth.

"A man like your father, Alan, a proud man but an angry man, would never have let me through the door if he thought I was carrying another man's child."

She was right of course. Although it had been easy to believe the issue was never discussed between them in the years that followed, like so many dark secrets in our house, it made no sense whatsoever that my father would not have confronted her when she learned she was pregnant with me. His pride would never have allowed him to stay silent.

So it became clear that at some point later, who knew when, he had decided it was the truth.

I absolutely believe that my father had not made up this tale as an attempt to hurt me, or derail my life, although he had succeeded at both. It was too multi-layered and complex a deceit for that to ring true. Also, and this was both a revelation and an arrow to my heart, I knew he didn't care enough about me to go to such elaborate lengths.

It became clear that this myth had been hatched to benefit only one person: himself. Somewhere along the line, my father had decided this was true to make himself feel better about the way he was treating my mother, and the way he was abusing me. Of course the awful, glaring flaw in this logic is that he had also been a monster to Tom too. It didn't make sense. But of course it shouldn't and it couldn't. I was trying to fathom my father's psychopathic behaviour that was based on a huge delusion. Surely it was not a big leap to think he might have found his own logic to merit Tom's abuse too? But every night, just as sleep began to smooth out the rattling of my brain, I would return to the same thought: I couldn't believe I was related to him. Maybe I had wanted it to be true so much, maybe that wish had actually seeped into my psyche, but now I couldn't accept that I was his son. And although I was, I most certainly was, I had the documents to prove it, I knew with every fibre of my being that there was nothing aside from blood that related him to me. And that's what kept me going. I may have been a robotic transvestite acting machine by day, and a preoccupied and cheerless dinner companion by night, but there was a light at the end of my tunnel: I was *not* my father's son.

SUNDAY 20TH JUNE 2010

I returned to New York and immediately dived into work. I was to perform in concert for a week at Feinstein's, Michael Feinstein's eponymous cabaret space at the Regency Hotel on the Upper East Side. I had played for a week there earlier in the spring to a great reception. I knew my song choices were probably a little idiosyncratic and certainly politically challenging for the club's regular demographic, but I believe if you're honest, true to yourself, and committed, and especially if you use humour as a tool as well as a balm, people will respect you perhaps more than if they agreed with everything you said. It's actually quite a good ethos for life: go into the unknown with truth, commitment and openness, and mostly you'll be okay.

I had started singing in concert like this only the year before. For years I had wanted to do a show of my own. On the rare occasions when I sang a song at a gala or benefit, not in character but as Alan Cumming, I was amazed at how different that felt. I wanted to pursue that feeling in more depth one day. But singing as myself brought with it many terrors. As I mentioned, I had no character to hide behind. I was singing as me. That felt like an enormous and terrifying leap to make, and that is why until not too long before, I rarely made it. I also had an added issue about singing in general. I can sing. I have sung often through the years in various plays and films, and many years ago actually released an album with my friend Forbes Masson as our comedy alter egos Victor and Barry. But I am not one of *those* singers. You know, the Broadwaaaaaaay belters, the beautiful singers. And even worse, since I have been on Broadway and even won a Tony award for Best Actor in a *Musical,* I felt that more and more people expected me to be one of *those* singers. They expected me to have that sort of polished sound. And I just don't. I don't want to, mind you, but one of the troubles with becoming more and more well known (and in this case well known for something you don't feel very confident about) is that you feel there is more and more of a chance you will disappoint.

I think also I was hampered by the perceived notion that actors like nothing better than to stand up in a crowded room and make a speech or sing a song. Both these activities, but especially the latter, would send me into paroxysms of panic and even with major rehearsal could induce severe, almost insurmountable nerves. So you can understand why it was an experience I wasn't in a hurry to repeat.

I'm not normally like that about acting. I'm usually quite relaxed about that, except for on opening nights.

And of course the more you do something, the more comfortable you become, and the less frightening it becomes. I realised that the only way to both conquer my fear and embrace my desire about singing was to accept a proposal my manager put to me to perform a concert in Lincoln Center's American Songbook series in February 2009.

And I was right. The more I did it, the more relaxed I became and the better I got. The more relaxed and the better I got, the more I did it. Nowadays I hop up onstage regularly to sing a song or duet with someone, and though I still get nervous, it's the good kind of nerves, the necessary kind, that keeps you on your toes and makes sure the adrenaline is flowing.

That first night, though, at the Allen Room of Jazz at Lincoln Center, a beautiful hall with enormous glass windows overlooking Columbus Circle and Central Park, I was very far from relaxed. My manager came to my dressing room to see how I was before the first show and I told her I wanted to punch her.

Ninety minutes later I was euphoric. I had done it! I had felt the fear and done it anyway. And I had enjoyed it and so had the audience, and best of all, I had felt that *connection*. The rawest, purest connection you can only feel when you let the audience see inside you. I was hooked. Next stop was the Sydney Opera House as part of the Mardi Gras festival, followed by runs at the Vaudeville Theatre in London's West End and the Geffen Playhouse in Los Angeles. Yes, I have always believed in starting small.

And now here I was, back at Feinstein's, singing a song I'd written about my disdain for plastic surgery to a room filled with people, many of whom had obviously had plastic surgery; telling stories about what I thought was the essential American experience— being on an M&M's float in the Macy's Thanksgiving Day Parade; then singing a searing, biting diatribe against all that is American, written by my musical director, Lance Horne; then asking the audience to contribute to a campaign to eject state politicians who had voted against marriage equality; before finishing with a rousing ditty with the chorus *"You're fucking beautiful, and when I kiss your lips I hear those fucking angels sing."*

You get the gist. It defined eclectic and it was exactly what

I needed. Each night I walked out onto the tiny stage and for ninety minutes my mind and my body were completely disengaged from what I'd just been through. The days were spent quietly, resting and walking our dogs in Central Park. Grant and I had decided to stay in a suite in the hotel that housed Feinstein's, as in a week I'd be off again to complete my turn on *Who Do You Think You Are?* and going up and downtown each day in the New York heat seemed unnecessarily exhausting. So every night, after the show, I could just pop back through the kitchens, up the service lift, and head back to my suite, and my husband, and true comfort.

Each night Grant and I would have drinks there with the friends who had come to the show, and each night I would recount the stories of Tommy Darling and of Alex Cumming, the two men who so completely filled my waking hours. It felt good to talk. Everyone was amazed by what I had to say. Their questions were thought provoking and sometimes allowed me new insight into what I had discovered. But mostly I felt solidarity and support and love, ironically three things I never felt from my father and three things I think Tommy Darling could have done with a whole lot more of.

SUNDAY 27TH JUNE 2010

When I arrived at Newark airport on Sunday morning I was told my flight to Beijing had been delayed and I would miss my connection to Kuala Lumpur. I was supposed to have arrived there on Monday afternoon, and had an evening and a good night's sleep to acclimatise myself and prepare for filming beginning on Tuesday. Now, alas, I would not arrive till Tuesday morning and would have immediately to start filming as soon as I landed, never an ideal situation, but certainly not when you're going to be on camera *sans* grooming after traveling for a day and a half!

I managed to call Elizabeth, the director, and she eased my qualms by saying that the first day of filming was pretty light anyway, and all I'd be doing was examining a few documents in the hotel. There was nothing left to do but enjoy the luxury of the Air China lounge. As a self-confessed airline-lounge whore, I had no problem with that at all.

In this bubble, this fancy no-man's-land, I found myself decompressing after a week of cabaret and confession. I brought my mind back round to my grandfather and the outcome of his story, which I knew was going to be explosive. As much as I was eager to solve the mystery of how he died, I was also wary of what I might learn.

TUESDAY 29TH JUNE 2010

I began filming in a hotel room overlooking the myriad beauties of Kuala Lumpur, which were, this morning, being drenched by a huge thunderstorm. From our sky-top vantage point we could see the dark clouds careening towards us, and the lightning reflecting across the dozens of glass towers we looked down upon.

Elizabeth's assurance that the first bit of filming would be "light" buoyed me as I struggled with jet lag and the crew set-up. On a table in front of me were some official-looking documents, facedown until the cameras would roll.

It was nice to see everyone again. I'd only known these people for one week before our month-long hiatus, but it was quite a week in terms of what we'd all gone through together, and being back amongst them felt comforting. And suddenly the next week and the inevitable bombshell of Tommy Darling's demise felt less daunting.

That feeling was not to last long. As the cameras began to roll,

I turned over the first document. It was Tommy Darling's death certificate.

It had come from the Malaysian National Archive. It read,

> ORIGINAL CERTIFICATE OF DEATH. POLICE LIEUTENANT T. DARLING. CAUSE OF DEATH: G.S. WOUND IN HEAD.

G.S., gunshot, wound in head. I went on to the autopsy report . . .

> ON 22ND JUNE 1951 AT 8 A.M. I PERFORMED AN AUTOPSY ON THE BODY OF AN ADULT MALE EUROPEAN IDENTIFIED BY P.C. 10112 AS T. DARLING, POLICE LIEUTENANT, AGED 35 YEARS. THERE WAS ONE GUN-SHOT WOUND OF ENTRY ABOUT THREE INCHES BEHIND AND LEVEL WITH THE RIGHT EAR. THERE WAS NO CHARRING OF THE SKIN. THE OCCIPITAL LOBES OF THE BRAIN WERE GROSSLY LACERATED AND A VERY MISSHAPEN BULLET WAS RECOVERED FROM THE LEFT OCCIPITAL LOBE OF THE BRAIN. CAUSE OF DEATH: SHOCK AND HEMORRHAGE FROM GUN-SHOT WOUND OF HEAD.

Brutal. I was so unprepared for this. If today was "light", what was the rest of the week going to be like?!

> ONE GUN-SHOT WOUND OF ENTRY ABOUT THREE INCHES BEHIND AND LEVEL WITH THE RIGHT EAR.

This was all wrong. I'd been told he'd died in an accident while cleaning his gun. But you don't clean your gun by pointing it to the side of your head. And then another thought struck me.

You don't kill yourself like that either. Had my grandfather been murdered?

What was going on here?

As if on some supernatural cue, a huge, deafening clap of thunder exploded across the sky. I leapt out of my seat.

The fact that there had been no charring of my grandfather's skin could only mean that he was shot at extremely close range, and the fact that the bullet entered the back of his head suggested he was executed in some paramilitary manner. Suddenly, finding the truth about Tommy Darling's end seemed menacing, and not at all liberating as I had hoped.

I had been given some information about Cha'ah, the village where Tommy had been stationed. Because of its position on the main route through the country of Malaya, it had become a hot spot for terrorist activity and was policed twenty-four hours a day by my grandfather's security force. I feared that Tommy Darling had met a vicious and violent end at the hands of the Maoist insurgents, possibly in a raid on his police station. What a sad and lonely way and place to die, I thought.

That night, I dreamt vividly of Tommy Darling and the horrors he must have faced in his dying moments. In my dream he was blindfolded, on his knees, hands tied behind his back, as a young, skinny, trembling Malayan boy held a gun to the back of his head. Everyone was screaming and panic-stricken, but Tommy Darling was stoically calm, except for a single tear that slid out from behind his blindfold and plopped down unnoticed onto the jungle floor.

WEDNESDAY 30ᵀᴴ JUNE 2010

I awoke sweating and disoriented at 4:30 A.M. I couldn't get back to sleep. I didn't really want to. I got up, did some yoga, but that didn't help. I decided to go for a walk. The sun was just beginning to peek out over the horizon. The gardens of this hotel were lush and airy, with pools at either end, and beyond the perimeter fence the jungle in all its primal, fertile plenty beckoned.

I thought of my grandfather standing here looking out at this natural bounty, this explosion of nature.

This is the air he would have breathed, I thought.

It was beautiful. It was magical.

I thought of what his life must have been like back in St Albans, all frost, loneliness, twitching net curtains and mean little hedges. No wonder he came back here, where there was this, where he was *someone*.

I swam in the pool. It felt good to be submerged. Under the water my jet lag had no purchase. I was the lone survivor in a post-apocalyptic paradise.

As I stretched out on a chaise, contemplating what my day would reveal to me, a door to the main building behind me creaked open and a little man carrying a huge bundle of towels appeared. I watched him as he struggled towards me, his face peeping out from behind his load from time to time, checking that he was still on the right path.

He arrived at his station and dropped the towels into a basket, then picked up one and came over to me brandishing it with both hands and a little bow.

"You have jet lag," he said with a smile.

"Yes," I replied. "How do you know?"

"Only jet lag people swim at five thirty!" he responded.

I laughed.

"You will have beautiful day," he said, starting to back away.

"I hope so," I replied quietly, and smiled.

"No need to hope," he said over his shoulder. "Many happy things will happen to you today."

And then he was gone and I was alone again. I shivered and wrapped myself up in the towel and made my way back to my room.

After breakfast we travelled to Cha'ah and I was taken to an old colonial-style country clubhouse, complete with elephant-hoof side tables and various stuffed animal heads mounted on the walls. Outside was a pool, glimmering in the baking sun. I wanted to jump in. I wanted to do anything other than do what I was about to do.

At the other end of the room was an old English military man, who I had been told had served with my grandfather in the Malayan police force. His name was Roy Samson, and the second I saw him I felt impending doom. Elizabeth was intentionally keeping Roy away until the crew was ready and we were set up on a terrace outside. Then I sat listening to him regale me with tales of killing young Communist guerrillas during jungle patrols. The relish with which Roy remembered these details did not sit easily with me, and I interrupted him impatiently for information about my grandfather.

Poor Roy, he had the air of a man who no longer got the opportunity to spout forth very often, and now, given the chance, he was doing so with loquaciousness and even glee.

"When we killed somebody, they were brought back to the police station for display to the public for two reasons. First of all, they had to be identified, and secondly, we wanted the local population to see what happens to terrorists, to give them a deterrent, in fact, from joining them. Now these are a couple of pictures of those *decorations* to the police station, if I may use the term, and they became the responsibility of Tom."

He laid out some pictures on the raffia drinks table between us. They showed the lifeless bodies of young Asian men laid out on the ground, and just behind them, squatting in a semi-circle, beaming proudly for the camera as though these young men were antelope or some other big game catch they had just taken in sport, were the British officers and their guides. Roy was amongst them. I was truly disgusted. I paused for a few moments. I wanted to get up and walk away from this man. I knew that his purpose here was to tell me something shocking about the death of my grandfather. But the way he was casually tossing down in front of me photographs of people he had killed made me worry that he would be as cavalier and insensitive about Tommy Darling's end. My stomach had started to churn. The jet lag was kicking in again. All I wanted to do was jump into that pool that sparkled behind me.

I gritted my teeth and held up another picture. In the foreground was a young man's contorted body, his eyes closed, his mouth agape. Poor Tommy Darling, who had been sent to De-olali to recover from the mental damage the horrors of jungle warfare had inflicted on him, was now once more face-to-face with the worst that mankind could inflict: death, and humilia-tion, and hubris.

Roy told me that this picture had been taken just outside the Cha'ah police station. These bodies were literally dumped on my grandfather's doorstep.

I sat back in my chair, stunned, my mind swirling.

I looked over at Elizabeth. She nodded. We'd discussed ear-lier that I should procure from Roy some general background on what life was like in the village. When I thought I'd heard enough, I would ask the question I was dying to have answered.

I steeled myself.

I asked Roy to tell me how my grandfather had died. I hoped the look on my face made it clear to him that I needed him to go easy.

"Well, realise that I wasn't there when Tom did die, so I can only tell you what the story was at the time. And that was that he was playing Russian roulette."

He kept talking, but my world stopped. My brow furrowed in incomprehension, and then I reeled backwards in my chair, try-ing to get as far away from Roy Swanson and his horrible news as I could, just as I had reeled back from my brother six weeks before on my roof deck in London.

Russian roulette? *Russian roulette?!*

I put both my hands to my forehead as though to shield my mind from more damage in Roy's incessant barrage. Then I smiled. The smile of a man who thinks there is nothing worse that he could ever hear.

I was suddenly very aware of the camera that was mere feet

from my face. This was the bargain, of course. I had finally got to the bottom of the mystery of my grandfather's death, but now the world would get to see me distraught, vulnerable, real. This was truly reality TV. And Roy kept talking.

"I can tell you now that he certainly had absolutely no reason that we knew of to deliberately kill himself. And the conclusion that I arrive at personally was that he either got careless, or he ran out of luck, or both."

My eyes began to fill with tears, but I didn't have time for that yet. I needed to stop Roy and get some things clear.

"Russian roulette? People played that?" I managed.

"You feed a round into one chamber of a revolver—" Roy began.

"Oh, I know what it is, I know," I interrupted.

"And you put it to your head. I'm told that somebody who is accustomed to doing it can tell by the feel of the pistol whether the round's at the top, opposite the barrel, or whether it's down at the bottom."

I nodded for too long, and too quickly, doing my best to remain calm.

"But was it a common thing to do, to play Russian roulette here?" I asked.

"I think it was for Tom. He had a reputation. The story was that he'd been playing it regularly for quite some time. My CO knew about it, he told us about it, and Tom's own immediate senior would've known about it. And the only conclusion I can arrive at is that Tom was so highly thought of as a police officer that they turned a blind eye to it."

My heart was pounding. All I could think about was Mary Darling. I have to tell this to Mary Darling.

"I'm sorry to have to say that to you," he continued.

I was taken aback by his sudden kindness.

"Oh, don't worry. Don't worry. I want to know," I replied. I lied, just a little.

"And, as I say," he continued, the brief sliver of tenderness he had shown gone forever, "I wasn't holding his hand at the time it happened."

I didn't judge Tom Darling for a second. I just tried to put it all together in a logical way. The photos, and the way Roy had talked about killing those men, those decorations, as he'd put it, I couldn't relate to that kind of chaos. If that was your reality, I think you'd have a completely different attitude about the value of life, including your own.

Mostly, I was just sad that my grandfather had met his end alone, never knowing the emptiness he would leave behind. His life meant so little to him then that the thought probably never occurred to him.

We had a sombre lunch in the main room of the club. I stayed at the other end of the table from Roy and ate in silence. I had taken Elizabeth to one side before the meal and asked her if there were to be any more shocks or sad news later in the day.

"To be honest," I'd said, "I'm feeling really shaky and I don't know if I can deal with any more revelations."

She looked at me kindly. "There will be some revelations," she began.

I gasped and dropped my gaze to the ground.

"But you'll be very pleased about them. Don't worry," she concluded.

It's really hard to talk about being famous. We live in a society that is obsessed with it, that ranks it as the best thing you could possibly achieve in your life.

I believe social media outlets like Facebook and Twitter are an absolute product of this obsession, as they partly manufacture how it feels to be famous for people who are not. You put personal information and images out into the world and the more friends or followers you obtain, the less knowledge you have of who is watching or keeping track. It's great to feel popular of course, but there is a downside.

Even so, most people, even friends who are close to you and privy to some of the more invasive aspects of fame, think the positive aspects far outweigh the negative and you shouldn't grumble but thank your lucky stars when blessed by the fame fairy. And to a certain degree they are right. Being famous is mostly great. I have a really amazing life. I get to do a job I really like and I get paid really well for it and I am loved. Because I am famous I have a voice and I can help effect change. And I get loads of free stuff.

But.

I am constantly self-conscious. Every day I spend large amounts of time meeting or talking to people I would rather not engage with. I sometimes fear for my physical safety. Let's leave it at that.

In the run-up to filming *Who Do You Think You Are?* I thought how lucky I was to have at my disposal all these resources and teams of researchers, to be able to give this gift to my mother of solving this family mystery. I said several times that this was in fact the best thing that had ever happened to me about being famous, and I truly meant it.

But right now, it wasn't looking like the best thing any more. Quite the reverse, in fact. I thought back to the telegram Granny had received. It was true. Tommy Darling had died in a shooting accident. I thought of the upset I was going to have to cause when I told my mother and my uncles what kind of accident it really was, and I wished at that moment that I'd never started this odyssey.

I felt so selfish. This was my search, and now they would have to deal with the consequences.

But then I thought of the other quest I had been on just now. I thought about the lesson I had taken away from my father's horrible chronicle and realised how important it is to be open, how the truth is all. And my Tommy Darling quest had been to find the truth as well. It was just that the truth was really painful right now.

After lunch I was driven into the actual village of Cha'ah, now no longer a village but a bustling little town with no indications of the perilous past its denizens once endured. I was to meet two local men who had known Tommy Darling. They were brothers named Datuk Rahman and Haji Ali and had been children at the time my grandfather had been here. Their father had been the head of the Malay community in Cha'ah then and a very good friend of Tommy Darling's. As I walked up the path to their front door I had a strange awareness that I was walking into a house that Tommy Darling had visited many times.

I took my shoes off and left them on the porch before knocking on the screen door. Two little, grinning old men approached me, hands outstretched. Immediately I felt safe. We sat in the cool of their living room and they told me of their memories of my grandfather.

"All the villagers at the time call him, in Malay, 'Tuan Darling.' 'Tuan' in Malay is 'Sir'," said Datuk Rahman, smiling at me through his thick-lensed glasses.

"Every morning he used to drive at ten o'clock all the way around." His arm shot up and traced a circle above his head. "And then another in the afternoon, all around." Again he made the circle. "When he driving around, he see the children. 'Tuan Darling! Tuan Darling!' we all cried."

I could feel both the men's empathy for me, and also a sense of hope that indeed they had something to share with me that would soothe my pain.

"I mean the feeling of the people was they love him very much," Datuk Rahman continued.

I wanted to know why the people of this town came to like Tom Darling so much, especially since he was there only a short time before he died.

"Well, he's the one who used to mix up all the gangs," said Datuk Rahman. "The leaders of the community, like my father, and a few others like the Chinese leader and Indian leader, they used to go together and have a good time. You know? They enjoyed drinking." So, Tuan Darling liked a party and a wee drink. I could relate.

Then I told the brothers that I had learned today how my grandfather had died. Their smiles quickly faded and their heads bowed in respect.

They told me how they had come to find out. It had been an extraordinarily hot day. There was a river at the edge of the village, still within what had been the perimeter fence, and they had gone there to swim and had seen a man they knew to be my grandfather's assistant at the police station washing a bloody sheet in the water. They asked him what he was doing and he told them it was the sheet that had been wrapped around the head of their precious Tuan Darling as he was rushed to hospital in the vain attempt to save his life.

I could see that after all these years, the vision of that bloody sheet still haunted these lovely old men. We sat in silence for a moment.

"Your father was very close with my grandfather," I continued. "He must've been very upset."

"Yes," nodded Haji Ali sadly.

"Yes," agreed his brother. "That's why he himself put up the road name, the 'Darling'."

I was incredulous. They had named a road after my grandfather? I couldn't quite fathom exactly why I was getting so moved by a road sign, but I was.

"Yes. Darling Walk," smiled Datuk Rahman.

"Darling Walk," repeated his brother.

"Darling Walk?" I asked again, as though I couldn't believe such a beautiful thing could have happened after all I had heard today.

"The local leaders here respect him, very high respect," said Datuk Rahman, very seriously.

"He'd done a good job."

I smiled at both the men and thanked them. They could not possibly know how much that last sentence resonated with me. All through my childhood, as I toiled my way through the exhaustive, insurmountable series of tasks my father would set me, I would dream that the conclusion of my work would be not the silent inspection followed by the inexorable spiral into anger and the force of his hand propelling me off balance. I dreamt that one day I would not be hit, and over his shoulder as he walked away from me I would hear my father say the words:

"You did a good job".

I felt connected to Tommy Darling in ways that went beyond our common lineage. We both lacked the same thing in our childhoods—the love of a father. For different reasons, of course, but it was a shared experience nonetheless. We both sought to fill that lack in our adult lives with family and love, as everyone does, but also with thrills and sometimes periods of recklessness. Luckily, I have always come back from my recklessness. Tommy Darling did not. But I also recognised restlessness in his spirit, a need to challenge himself, that I too have experienced throughout my life. I wondered, if I didn't have the job I have, which provides me with such thrilling, visceral release, would I be seeking those thrills in destructive ways? I know I love the rush of adrenaline pulsing through my veins. I wonder to what lengths I would go to experience it if I didn't do what I do?

We left the brothers' house, and I walked with them into the centre of town, where I discovered that there was not only a road named after Tommy Darling, but a park as well. The brothers proudly showed me the sign that said "Darling Walk" and we walked along the little paved road and round the "Darling Walk Recreational Park". There was a kids' playground, trees, people strolling happily. It all seemed right.

The horrifying news of this morning was tempered by these new revelations. To be able to tell my mum that all these years there had been a park and a road on the other side of the world bearing her father's name would be a sweet antidote to the shock of how he had met his end. It actually seemed so fitting that even at the very end of his life Tommy Darling touched those around him. He was a reckless man, inscrutable, but magnetic too.

None of us had known that he had gone to Buckingham Palace to receive his Military Medal, but he had. None of us, till now, knew that he was so beautifully memorialised, but he was. He had made a huge impression on these people. He was obviously a very charismatic man.

Once we'd made our little stroll the brothers took me to the exact spot where the shooting had actually happened.

"This is the place," said Datuk Rahman soberly.

"This is it," said Haji Ali.

"The coffee shop is there," the first brother continued, pointing across the street to a little store. "They took the beer, bring to this tent."

He drew an imaginary line around the perimeter of the tent that had been set up in the town square fifty-nine years ago. I pictured Tommy Darling and his cohorts finishing their patrol, getting a beer, and walking across the street for some shade in the tent. Then . . . what? I didn't want to imagine the rest. Not here, not as I stood on the very spot. I looked around me. There was a little girl coming down the slide in the playground, and another clambering into a swing.

It was lovely to see those children playing in the place where something so horrible had happened.

"Your grandfather is a hero, you know. We respect him, very highly respect," said Datuk Rahman, patting my arm gently with his hand.

I got in the car alone. The crew had to stay behind, and I had a long trip back. I was glad to have the time to myself. I needed some time where nobody spoke to me, and nobody showed me or told me anything monumental or life changing. I was utterly drained. Thinking ahead, Elizabeth had made sure there was a bottle of wine in the back seat of the car. It was just what I needed.

I said my good-byes to the brothers, vowing to return one day with my mother to show her this memorial to the man they so revered. I opened the bottle and raised a glass to Darling Walk as it passed by me in the dusk. And then my thoughts returned to the man himself, the man who had lived life with the volume cranked way, way up. I felt filled with love and admiration for him.

"Here's to you, Tommy Darling," I said, a little teary. "You did a good job."

THURSDAY 1ST JULY 2010

The next day I found myself in the Malaysian National Archives, a grand series of buildings nestled on a hill above Kuala Lumpur, where amid the hushed corridors I was told I would find documented proof to back up the revelations about my granddad's death.

I was ushered into a grand library by a gentle lady named Gowri. She disappeared to find the relevant files while the crew set up in silence.

Today I felt strangely calm. I knew the worst was over. I knew that the next day we would be flying to neighbouring Singapore to visit Tommy Darling's grave, but today felt like a buffer between the shock of yesterday and the finality of tomorrow.

Gowri returned and gently placed a thick folder of documents in front of me. It was labeled L773. Lieutenant T. Darling.

The first document I saw was a police telegram that detailed exactly the events of 22nd June 1951.

> Darling and Police Lieutenant Macdonald returned to Cha'ah from patrol 12 noon, entered coffee shop for refreshment, and were joined by Assistant Resettlement Officer. Darling asked Assistant Resettlement Officer for loan of his .38 revolver, took 5 rounds from chamber leaving one, spun chamber, held revolver to head, behind ear, and pulled trigger. You will recognise this as old game called Russian roulette. Striker hit the single round which discharged killing Darling instantaneously.

I let the thin piece of paper slip from my hands.

Next I saw some correspondence between the Malayan police force and my granny. Immediately my stomach clenched and I felt a lump in my throat. I thought of her, the laughing, joy-filled character who had always encouraged me to be naughty, to be reckless, to be myself. Now I wondered if she'd seen something of her husband in the little boy she'd spoiled all those years ago.

> **Dear Mrs. Darling, may I express to you on behalf of all ranks of the Force our sincere sympathy in the sad loss of your husband. Thomas was handling a revolver and by an unfortunate mischance he fired a shot which caused his own instantaneous death.**

The letter went on to relay the particulars of his funeral, how many ceremonial shots had been fired, how many floral tributes. I kept looking at the paper and breathed in a deep, strengthening breath.

Of course. They didn't tell my granny what really happened. How could they?

I thought how sensitive it had been of them to have kept the true horror from her and her kids. Then I saw the next letter in the paper trail.

It was from Granny.

I recognised her handwriting from birthday cards and notes she sent me over the years. I have the last one she ever sent to me framed on my bookshelves, so I was very familiar with her penmanship.

> Dear Sir, about your inquiry as to how I would like to dispose of my husband's effects, I would like ever so much to get them sent home ...

My eyes began to fill with tears and my throat closed up at the thought of her sitting down to write this letter, the very letter I held in my hands now.

> ... as the children would like something belonging to him as a keepsake, also myself, as we have nothing of his to remember him by.

My poor dear Granny. The man she had loved, but with whom it hadn't worked out, had died on the other side of the world and she had nothing palpable to make sense of it.

I thought of how the story of Tommy Darling's death had been passed down to me. Obviously the vagueness of the Malayan police force's explanation had been slightly augmented or embellished over the years. I began to think back to the few occasions when it had been mentioned and the variations I had heard. I also remembered the way the whole incident was referred to in slightly hushed tones, partly not to upset Granny but also, as I now remembered, as there was a feeling of some wrongdoing on the authorities' behalf in the way Granny had been treated.

Then I read a series of internal memos dealing with the issue of my grandfather's officer's pension, and eventually, after much toing and froing and a desultory mention of "the widow", I saw to my horror the ratification of the decision not to award my granny her rightful widow's pension, the pension that, though separated, Tommy Darling still wanted her to have.

The reason they gave for withholding this lifeline to my family was that his death was not the way it was *envisaged* in some subsection of the Malayan police rule book to merit it.

Out of nowhere came memories of stories of my granny having to work so many jobs in the fields of the farms around where she and her four kids lived, scrabbling to get by, suddenly plunged into poverty after the support her husband had always provided her stopped overnight.

There were a few more letters from Granny enquiring about the pension and when it would commence, and how she had had to borrow money and also agree to a temporary loan from the state to cover her family's expenses. Then the letters stopped. She must have got the message. She realised the pension was not coming, if not the reason why.

Anger bubbled up inside me. Tommy Darling had worked hard for his country all his life. He had risked his life many times; indeed it was a miracle he hadn't been killed in battle. Now, the very military system he had supported and upheld, that had made him the man he was, was punishing him and his family for the results of the circumstances he had endured. For I had no doubt that the reason Tommy Darling blew his brains out in that tent that sunny morning nearly sixty years before was because of the trauma he had suffered on the fields of war. He was undiagnosed, untreated, but the man was ill.

Still riled, I moved on to some correspondence from a year later with a letterhead from the police department in Elgin, a town near my granny's home in Scotland. Apparently a sergeant from the station had been asked by the commissioner of police back in Malaya to go and interview Granny, perhaps because she'd moved and they couldn't contact her. He wrote:

> I interviewed her there and she states that she is the widow of the Police Lieutenant who died in Malaya in 1951. Mrs. Darling added that a box containing her late husband's property has been lying at Liverpool docks for a year . . .

I lifted my hand to my forehead as if to keep inside the sadness I knew was bursting to get out at what I had seen in the next part of the sentence:

> . . . as she is unable to pay the four pounds carriage demanded.

Tears ran down my face.

I cried for my granny and my mum and every working-class woman who had sacrificed like them and been denied proper closure and emotional balm because they had slipped through the system, no, had been *failed* by the system, and hadn't the means to do so.

I blew out several breaths of sadness before I was eventually able to continue.

"Oh, my poor little granny. That's so tragic."

I dropped my head into my hands and just cried for a bit. All that I had been through in the last six weeks, from that revelation on the roof in London to the bombshell of yesterday converged in that library in an emotional dead end. And for all the horrors of Tommy Darling's story and the dredging up of the past the sudden re-entry of my father into my life had caused, it was this detail, this horribly human detail of a mere four pounds that got to me the most.

Life can be so fucking bleak, I thought.

Imagine then how heartened I was to read the next letter, which recorded how the Malayan police had sent a postal order to my granny to pay for the shipping of the property. That was the least they could do.

I've been thinking a lot lately about how a man I never knew putting a gun to his head in a town on the other side of the world over sixty years ago had such an impact on my attitude towards money, and in fact the whole way I live my life.

We all learn lessons from our parents, of course, and they from theirs. But perhaps more importantly we glean our wisdom from our circumstances and our feelings of security, or lack thereof. Mary Darling was a girl of thirteen when her life was turned upside down, sending her and her siblings into hardscrabble poverty. I think I learned from her that having money could never be guaranteed. It could disappear at any moment. And so I have grown up wanting to feel secure when it comes to money, but doing so by treating it as something to be enjoyed, shared, and not given power. I guess I could have gone the other way and become one of those people who define themselves by their wealth. But I honestly believe that I have taken the knowledge that things can change in an instant, and made it key to my philosophy of life: neither money nor my work define me. I like them, they allow me to do many things I enjoy, but if I did not have them, I know

I would be able to find something else to do, I would be able to survive, I could be happy.

Sometimes the worst thing about change is the shock of the change itself and not actually the new circumstances. Perhaps because of Tommy Darling, genetically and through his legacy, I embrace change, I never take anything for granted, and I never forget how lucky I have been, and am.

THURSDAY 1ˢᵀ JULY 2010, EVENING

L ater that day we all went to the Coliseum Café. This was an old colonial hangout where military personnel travelling through Kuala Lumpur to their positions elsewhere in the country would have congregated. Again I was in a place Tommy Darling would almost certainly have been. The bar didn't look like anything had changed much since his time. The yellow peeling walls were packed with pictures of military types in formal gear as well as framed newspaper articles about various important issues to the clientele like "When Your Servant Has Malaria!"

I got a beer and sat in the window watching the world go by as the crew set up, enjoying the feeling of nearness, thinking about how he must have sat here sipping a drink and looking out on this same street. My odyssey was nearly over but I knew it would resonate with me for a very long time. I began to wonder how Tommy Darling would have fared in the present, if he were a soldier now in Afghanistan or Iraq, how different his life would have been. I remembered the article I'd read in the middle of the night before, jet-lagged and fixated on his story and how to best couch it all to my mum. Although combat stress, or post-traumatic stress disorder, is now recognised by the military as a medical condition, there is still a huge amount of stigma attached to it by all sections of society, and there is no significantly successful treatment. Sadly, the article went on to say that suicide is the leading cause of death for members of the U.S. Army today, which has seen its rates double since 2004. Maybe Tommy Darling wouldn't have fared so well today either.

But as I downed the last of my beer I determined to do something when I returned home, a fund-raiser, some sort of memorial in Tommy's honour that would benefit a PTSD organisation, in the hope that someone, somewhere would get the help he never did.

"His death is not so shocking when you look at his life," I began when the crew was set up.

Elizabeth asked if I felt I'd learned anything about myself. I stared into space and thought for a moment.

"Finding out about him and having to share that with my mum and my family has kind of reinforced my belief that it's really important to be honest and open and to have no skeletons in the closet. Cos, you know, the truth can hurt, but not knowing can hurt more."

I wasn't talking just of Tommy Darling of course. The two parts of this story now seemed so clearly connected, mirroring each other perfectly. I had lost a father but found a grandfather. One of them had never sought the truth and lived a life based on a lie; the other's truth was hidden from us because society deemed it unsuitable. Both caused strife, and sadness. But now, both combined to reinforce for me what I knew to be the only truth: there is never shame in being open and honest.

It was shame that prevented us from knowing what a great man Tommy Darling was. And it was shame that made my father treat me and Tom and my mum the way he did.

All those years ago, lying in the grass of the forest at Panmure, I rejected shame instinctively. Now my forefathers had reinforced for me how right I had been all along.

FRIDAY 2ND JULY 2010

The next day we made the short flight from Kuala Lumpur to Singapore and then drove to Kranji Cemetery, where Tommy Darling was buried. As we walked through the large stone sentry gates that guard the grounds, I remembered how excited Mary Darling had sounded when I told her this was to be the conclusion of my journey, and I vowed I would walk through these gates again one day with her.

There is a white cross-shaped memorial in the centre with a large tower reaching out from it, and just past there and on to the right as far as you can walk is where I found my grandfather's final resting place.

I felt surprisingly happy. I had not lost anyone, I had found someone, and I was here to celebrate him. He was in a nice spot, under a big tree. I paid my respects, and it was all over.

I said my emotional good-byes to the crew at a restaurant before I was driven to the airport for the journey home. I was going to miss them. We'd been through a lot together, and I was grateful to them for the kindness they had shown me in a time of great need.

I flew from Singapore to Tokyo and then had a few hours' layover and once more was able to indulge in my lounge worship. But even this swanky Air Nippon lounge couldn't quite lift me out of the numbness that had descended. It was now Saturday morning around 8 A.M. My body clock was all over the place. I was drinking a sake Bloody Mary (I am very adaptable!) and Skyping with my assistant who was at my house in the Catskills, preparing for the influx of friends who were coming up for the Fourth of July holiday weekend. There the time was 8 P.M. the night before. As much as I was looking forward to seeing Grant and my friends, I was a little apprehensive. I felt like one of those soldiers returning from the battlefield a different man. I have a webcam on my house that looks out to the meadow and the rolling hills beyond. It's meant to be one of those security cameras that you face towards your house, but I like that it shows me what I look out at when I'm up there. If I feel needy of my life in the Catskills, it's only a couple of clicks away. You'd be amazed just how helpful and relaxing a few seconds staring at it on a computer screen can be.

That Saturday morning, or Friday night depending on your vantage point, I was able to watch my assistant and my friend Lance bouncing on the trampoline I have in the meadow. It was unreal to think that I would actually be there with them the following afternoon (or later that day). I was about to start one of those crazy journeys where I would arrive before I had departed. It was a good metaphor for how life felt for me around that time—surreal, out of control. Everything I had known as sure and true had been taken away, shaken up, and then recalibrated back into my life and I was supposed to carry on regardless. I guess I had no choice.

I knew I just needed to give it all time, let it sink in, let things settle, then reassess and see how I had changed.

For the moment I was going to have another sake Bloody Mary and a plate of edamame, then get on a plane and watch films with Sandra Bullock in them and cry.

Part Three

MOVING
ON

One of my favourite games is called "Two Truths and a Lie". You say three things about yourself, two of which are true, one of which is a lie, and the other players have to decide which is the lie. Well, you can imagine how great it was to be able to add "I recently discovered my grandfather died in Malaysia playing Russian roulette" to my arsenal of truths! Or how about "My father recently told me I wasn't his son, but he was lying"?!

All summer I found myself telling the story to practically everyone in whose company I spent more than a few minutes. I could not stop thinking or talking about it. I knew that, as with any traumatic happening, it was important to give it weight, to acknowledge the effect it must be having on me, and to use the talking about it as a way to cleanse my system. That way I would eventually be able to create some distance, and therefore some objectivity. That's the idea, anyway.

It's a bit like when you break up with someone and you can't stop talking about them until you get them out of your system.

Though of course, having known many friends who suffered from Compulsive Break-up Talking syndrome and unfortunately having suffered from it myself more than a few times, I knew the danger was that my Compulsive Familial Bombshell Talking syndrome could oh so quickly and easily develop into Boring Old Fart Who Just Can't Seem to Move On syndrome.

Although I'm joking, there were some similarities between my story and dealing with an ex. Or to be precise, dealing with two exes. My father was now definitively out of my life. I would never talk to him again. My grandfather too was gone, just as quickly and dramatically as he had appeared.

Both of them left many unanswered questions behind. Both were charismatic men with strong personalities and both had left their imprint on me on every level: emotionally, spiritually, genetically. Because of their absence I was a changed man, and talking about them and telling the story of my insane summer was my way of trying to realign myself and clear a path through the wreckage they had left behind them so I could move on.

I went back into therapy. One of the annoying things about starting with a new therapist, I have discovered over the years, is that you have to bring them up to speed on a lifetime's worth of your stories. And that can be quite time-consuming! But actually, considering the magnitude of what I had just been through, it was a good and useful exercise for me to go back through my childhood and early life and give it more context. It still took a while, though.

After a couple of months I said to my therapist at the end of a session, "I don't know why I'm here."

"What do you mean?" she said, her face at once inquisitive and perfectly calm.

"Well I mean I know why I'm here of course. I've just had a

huge fucking crazy lot of shit happen to me. But aside from that I sort of feel there's some other reason why I've needed to come and see you and I'm just not sure what it is."

I looked at one of the many clocks in the room. My time was up. I began to gather my things. After a moment she replied, "I think you're coming here because you know your father is dying and you want to make your peace with him."

I felt like I'd been slapped across the face. It was so obvious, and so right. That was exactly what I was doing.

"Yes," I said softly. "I think you're right." I went home and bawled my eyes out.

The date of the broadcast of my episode of *Who Do You Think You Are?* approached. Because of filming in New York I wasn't going to be able to watch it on the BBC with my mum as I'd hoped, but we were both sent a DVD. It lay in my bag for days before I had the courage to watch it. It felt like I was taking a chance on opening up a wound that had only just healed. And it certainly didn't pull any punches. There I was receiving the news that my grandparents had separated, that Tommy Darling's medical records had been removed due to the psychological damage he'd suffered, and eventually of course the gory and shocking details of the Russian roulette.

It was so strange to feel sorry for myself. The few months since, combined with the change in my physical appearance (my body hair had grown back in—I no longer resembled the pale, hairless man-child on the screen), had ensured that there was a healthy distance between the me then and the me now, so I could empathise with as well as relive the experience.

Also there was the experience of seeing myself completely off guard. Even in a show like this, where one is supposedly ignoring the cameras and the viewer is a fly on the wall, there is always of course some awareness of being filmed. Several times on my episode, all that was stripped away as I received information that completely floored me. I saw myself as I never truly have seen myself on-screen before: completely unadulterated, vulnerable and authentic. It was fascinating but not very pleasant.

I could tell Mum was very anxious about the show being broadcast. It's easy to forget how exposing being on television can feel at the best of times to people who aren't used to it, but having very personal details of your parents revealed publicly was something she had no experience of whatsoever.

In the end Mary Darling decided she wanted to watch the show alone, and spent the rest of the evening answering her phone, which was ringing off the hook with people from all parts of her life wanting to speak to her about what they'd just witnessed.

For the next few months, people contacted her constantly about Tommy Darling's story. Some she knew; others were strangers who had known him or known my granny. I think it was good for her. Much in the same way that I felt I had to keep telling my dual family narrative, she was able to talk it out in this way and was also fascinated to find out more details about the father she never knew. She has since met several relations from her father's family, and continues to explore both sides of our family tree, armed with all the initial research that was done for the show before they realised my grandfather's story was the one to focus on. I delivered to her two large binders bursting with documents, and she has had a field day with them.

I began to look into PTSD organisations with a view to arranging a charity screening of the programme in honour of my grandfather. I discovered one called Give an Hour that I decided to contact. The premise of this group was that mental health professionals would give free hourly increments of mental health services to veterans returning from Iraq and Afghanistan, and then in turn the people who received this free care would give an hour of their time to some form of community service.

I liked the way it was so simple and went straight to the heart of the problem, and also that the veterans who were receiving the care were also able to give something back in return.

I hoped that in some small way I would be able to help some people in need, ensuring that they were given the professional psychological care that was never available to my granddad. But that wasn't the only reason. I didn't quite know it at the time, but now I understand that this event was a gesture to my father too. The more I have talked about him and what happened in my past, with both friends and mental health professionals, the more I have come to believe that he too suffered from some undiagnosed mental condition. It's not just his violence, his volatility and mood swings, it's his complete lack of empathy, his seemingly utter inability to consider the feelings of anyone else. And of course my dealings with him over the course of that summer only underscore this. I was not talking to a sane man in those phone calls. There was a disconnect and an egotism that was at times breathtaking: his insistence that I must have known I was not his son all along. His question: "Did you not notice we never bonded?" And worst of all, the utter absence of an apology or any hint that he understood what he had put me through when I eventually was the one to break the truth to him. All these things regularly float through my mind and convince me of his madness.

I am not a psychologist (though I've spent a lot of time in their company!) and although I have speculated about what exactly my father's condition or conditions might have been, I am weary of it all, weary of the wondering. This much I know: the bene-fit screening I held at the Tribeca Grand Hotel on Sunday 7th November 2010 was a gesture to both Tommy Darling and Alex Cumming.

"This past summer has been really difficult for me, and so to-night is in some way a form of closure," I'd said in my speech before the programme was screened.

I had no idea just how much closure.

The next day I woke up to the news that my father had died that night.

THURSDAY 17TH FEBRUARY 2011

Once a year I go to Boston to record the introductions for *Masterpiece Mystery*, just to annoy Patti Smith. It's a fun annual jaunt. My assistant and my friend Michael, the groomer, had come up with me on the train from New York the afternoon before. That evening we had dinner with my old chum John Tiffany, who was doing a sabbatical at Harvard and so living in Boston at the time. John had directed me in *The Bacchae* for the National Theatre of Scotland. Soon we would begin work on our next project together, *Macbeth*.

After much mirth and a chilly walk back to the hotel in the snow, we were up bright and early the next day and at the WGBH studios to start shooting. I was sitting in the make-up chair checking my e-mails when I saw one from my brother.

Hi Alan. Hope all is well.
See the attached which you need to respond to.

That's odd, I thought. Tom wasn't usually so enigmatic. But then

I opened up the attachment and I saw why. Our father had once more, even from beyond the grave, entered our lives.

It was a letter to Tom from our father's solicitor.

My heart was thumping as I read it. The title in bold was "Your Late Father's Estate".

The man introduced himself as the person who had been dealing with the winding up of the estate and said he was writing with regard to our "potential Legal Rights claim."

I made as if to speak, but the whirr of Michael's hair dryer filled my ears, and anyway, I didn't quite know what to say. I had no idea what this could possibly mean. On the one hand I felt like I was suddenly a living manifestation of one of the plots of the *Mystery* shows I was about to introduce, and on the other I just couldn't believe that my father was still able to exert such an influence. He was the embodiment of those buried mines left long after a conflict had ended that occasionally erupt, and the pain of the past as well as the carnage of the present combine in a perfect storm.

As you know, your father left a Will in which neither yourself or your brother Alan was bequeathed any items.

The idea that my father would have left anything to us had never crossed my mind, though I had wondered if I would ever receive that letter he had spoken of, the one that originally would have been the harbinger of my true lineage. In the intervening months I had often thought how lucky I had been to have had the chance to talk to him and get to the bottom of all this whilst he was still alive, rather than be presented with a letter after his death. The idea that I would never have had the chance to question him, challenge him, and of course be able to tell him he was wrong was completely inconceivable to me now.

> Under the terms of Scots Law you are entitled to a share of
> your late father's estate irrespective of his Will. This share is
> called Legal Rights.

What?! Irrespective of his will?! Scotland has a law that over-
rules a father's will?

> Legal Rights are calculated by taking the net moveable estate
> (the moveable estate excludes any property such as houses
> or flats) and dividing it into two. One half share is made over
> under the terms of the Will and the second half forms what is
> known as the legitim or bairns' part.

It was all starting to come clear. "Bairns" is a Scottish word for
children. Basically my country, at some point in its history, saw fit
to enact a law to stop errant fathers from not providing for their
offspring after their own death.

> It is this share that is then divided between the number of
> children. In your father's case it would be divided between you
> and your brother Alan.

Over the next few days my brother and I were thrown into yet
another tailspin of my father's doing. We swung between thinking we should take the money—it was ours, after all, legally—and
then thinking that by taking it we would be in some way accepting blood money.

We truly felt that passionately and extremely about it. It wasn't
about the money, though obviously that was a nice surprise; it
was more the feeling of being beholden to someone we did not
respect, who had made it clear he did not respect or love us.

Both of us were so riled that we were so riled, and we knew our father would have loved to think of us spending so much time agonising over an edict of his.

Eventually I spoke to the solicitor.

"We haven't decided exactly what to do yet, but I wanted to ask you a couple of questions to clear a few things up," I began.

"Fire away!" he replied.

"Did my father know that this would be the outcome of his will? I mean would he have been told about this?" I asked.

"Absolutely," the lawyer said unequivocally. "He would have been told about the Legal Rights issue when he made his will."

"And so, even though he knew that we were entitled to half his financial estate, he still made a decision not to name us?" I was incredulous, and couldn't bear to think where this conversation was going.

"That is correct," the lawyer said.

"So he decided to actively keep us out of his written will in order that we would have to make the decision to take the money that was legally due us?" I responded.

"That would appear to be the case," came the reply.

I then called my father a name that I rarely use and do not approve of but in this case was the only appropriate moniker for such a loaded and manipulative and cowardly gesture.

So basically my dad *wanted* my brother and me to be having the dilemma we were having right now. It was one last blow to our hearts, one last fuck with our heads.

I could see my father's face as he was told the ramifications of making his will as he did. I saw him thinking of Tom and me being made to question and struggle and suffer as we interpreted his actions, and enjoying the prospect of us doing so.

That was it for me. After a short chat with Tom I called back the solicitor and told him we were taking the money. I was calling the old bastard's bluff.

I wanted him to be the provider, finally, of something positive in our lives. I wanted to use the cash to do something as a family that would be happy and meaningful and positive, and I knew exactly what that would be.

TWO YEARS LATER

Me, Grant, Tom and his wife, Sonja, and Mary Darling made what I suppose can only be called a pilgrimage to Malaysia, and retraced both my and Tommy Darling's steps.

We flew from London, and even after a seven-hour layover in Abu Dhabi we arrived not exhausted, but refreshed and lean, as we had slept the sleep of champions in our first-class pods and had massages in the lounges of both our ports of call. I could see, watching Mary Darling, where I got my lounge addiction from.

We had a driver, Khairy, who had been on the *Who Do You Think You Are?* shoot, and were helped by Alan D'Cruz, who had been the show's fixer, as it is called in filmy circles.

The first night we met up with Alan for drinks at the Coliseum Café, and I could see the gleam in my mother's eyes as she sat having a drink and imagining she was in a bar where her father had once been.

The next day we went to the Malaysian archives and were shown to a private room by the lovely Gowri. We pored over the correspondence detailing Tommy Darling's death and the ensuing stream of letters back and forth to Granny. Tom, Mum and I all marveled at the idea of seeing Granny's handwriting in a little room of an archive on the other side of the world. We found out more about Tommy Darling's life there, and again it was wonderful to see my mum so engaged with her father's legacy.

The next day we went down south towards Cha'ah and I knew to a part of the trip that might be very painful for my mother. I needn't have worried.

As we turned the corner into the street where Datuk Rahman and Raji Ali lived, I was shocked to see it so busy. Car after car was parked all around the house, and I saw a marquee and crowds of people all waving at us. I realised that these two little old men had got out the bunting, quite literally, for the arrival of the daughter of Tuan Darling.

The whole town seemed to have stopped. All the elders of the village were gathered for a feast at the brothers' home, and Mary Darling was the guest of honour. If she had not understood the magnetism and the legacy of her father, she must now, surrounded by people who, for the most part, had never known him but who had felt his influence and his charisma in the very fabric of their lives.

After lunch we went to the town square, walked along Darling Walk, and sat in Darling Recreational Park. The brothers told Mary Darling the details they had told me of that morning in 1951. I could see her try to maintain her composure. As fascinating and revelatory as all this was, and as kind and beautiful as these men were, she was still the little girl finally understanding where her father had been. At one point they wanted to take a picture of her at the very spot where he had shot himself. I could see her steel herself for it, not wishing to appear rude, but I could also instantly tell the toll it was taking just imagining the horror.

"Are you okay, Mum?" I asked.

"Yes," she gulped, unconvincingly.

"You don't have to take the picture if you don't want to."

She signalled to me she didn't, and I subtly but firmly broke the moment.

At a market I admonished my mum for constantly running off and then made her promise to tell us if she was going to go to a stall in another direction.

"I'm worried I'm going to lose you, Mum," I had said, and let it hang in the air for a moment before she nodded and we both knew that something had altered forever. It was as though Tommy Darling hung over us, and we were all made aware of the frailty of life, the importance of family, and the power of love.

Eventually we drove to Singapore, and it was there, after we all visited his grave, that I heard my mother say something that made my heart fly. It made me take heart to hear that I had done a good job in arranging this trip, but more importantly, that doing this TV show, in fact, being famous, was all worth it.

I had walked away from the grave and gone to stand under the nearby tree to take a video of everyone else leaving. I was shooting Grant and Mary Darling as they walked towards me, and just before they left my frame I heard my mother say,

"Well, they say dreams do come true . . ."

When we arrived back in New York, Grant made an observation.

"You know the best thing about this whole trip?" he asked.

"What?" I replied.

"Your father wasn't mentioned once!"

And it was true. We none of us ever mentioned him at all. Not through some desire to expunge him from this experience, not because we felt awkward that he was inadvertently paying for this amazing odyssey. No, none of that. We just didn't think of him. He wasn't that important to us. He no longer had any power over us.

Part Four

POSTSCRIPT

T hat was supposed to be the end, you know.

Under that tree, beneath a cloudless Singaporean sky, with Mary Darling walking past me saying her dream had come true, with the man I love accompanying her, and my amazing brother and sister-in-law following them. That was supposed to be the end of this book.

Then, about eight months later, just after Christmas 2012, Jack, my mum's companion for twenty-five years, died after a long illness. Grant and I flew to Scotland for the funeral.

The night before the funeral we all stayed over at Mary Darling's—me, Grant and Tom. At dinner I said that on our way back from Forfar, where Jack's funeral was, I'd like to go to Panmure Estate, have a drive around, and show Grant where I'd grown up.

I knew that over the years the estate had ceased to operate as I had known it. The farms and the plantations were divided up, the sawmill closed down, and the various workers' houses were sold off to whoever wanted them.

We entered from the east gates, late afternoon sun throwing long shadows of the leafless trees across our faces like a strobe machine.

It was so beautiful. I realised I had grown up in spectacular beauty but I hadn't noticed. I suppose my mind was elsewhere.

We drove the route that Tom and I had walked on that last visit with our father nineteen years before.

We stopped at the bridge and I hopped out of the car and ran the path along the top of the cliff, though it is too leafy and sloping to really call a cliff. I arrived at the stone engagement seat that some earl or other had built at some point for his fiancée to sit on during their courting walks through the forest. Grant ran behind me, trying to keep up, snapping away with his camera.

I felt so free. Isn't that funny? I felt at home and happy. This was not an emotion I had ever expected to feel that day.

The drives, once pristine and manicured, were now rowdy and overgrown.

As we drove down through the sawmill yard towards the house, the walk I'd feared twice every school day, I gasped repeatedly.

Everything had been knocked down. The sawmill was just a pillaged skeleton; the tractor shed a concrete square with weeds growing up through it.

I felt the *absence* of my father. He was order and neatness and spit and polish. This was utterly decrepit. He was gone. And so I felt able to observe my childhood home like I would a box of old photos I chanced upon in a cupboard.

The house was empty, but locked of course. It had apparently recently been purchased. A weekend home for some wealthy family, most likely.

It still felt big. I'd expected to find it less daunting now, but no, it was still bleak and menacing.

We walked round the unkempt garden and looked in the windows. It was just as I remembered it. There was the sink, the kitchen rearranged a bit but much the same, just a kitchen in a big stone house in the Angus countryside.

I saw the wee room off the living room where I'd played the piano.

The Good Room that we literally spent a handful of evenings in all year.

As I turned the corner into the house driveway I caught a glimpse of the silhouette of my father through the net curtain of the office window. My heart skipped a beat and I stopped.

Grant later told me how in the woods I'd run and leapt on stones and over fallen trees, but the closer we got to the house the slower I became, and more measured. Of course the woods meant freedom to me, air and imagination and being unobserved. The house was all darkness and silence and expecting the worst.

My hand was on the doorknob to the shed. I turned it open and walked inside. This was where, more than thirty years before, my irrational and irate father had held me down and clipped my hair with sheep shears.

I took in every crack of the stone floor, every nail banged into the crumbling plaster of the walls, until my gaze rested on what I realised was my reflection through the cobwebs in the window.

I smiled.

If my father had been alive I think he would probably have been quite proud of me right now.

I was wearing a tailored black suit, white shirt, and slim black tie, black brogues, my hair well cut and groomed. Even my glasses were clean.

I think my father would have approved of me. I think I would have finally passed his test.

But I had come back here, dressed like this, out of respect for Jack, not my father.

It didn't matter what he thought anyway.

I thought I looked just fine.

ACKNOWLEDGEMENTS

Jason Weinberg completely managed this whole thing, I now realise. Luckily he is my manager. It was he who got me to sit down with Luke Janklow in the café of the Standard Hotel in West Hollywood late one afternoon during a week of night shoots on a movie in the summer of 2011, much against my will, I might add. Then Luke was the one who completely surprised me by not exhorting me to do a "my fabulous celebrity life" type of book but to write about something I really felt passionate about. Luckily Luke is my agent. Through Luke I met Carrie Thornton, who encouraged me to go deeper and darker and to trust that my story was good enough. Luckily Carrie is my editor. I owe such a huge debt to all three.

If my childhood had been pleasant and uneventful, then even if in middle age Tommy Darling's story had been suddenly sprung on me as it was, I probably wouldn't have written a book. My family would all have gathered round the parental home's TV and watched the shocking tale unfold, and then I'd be pulled into the collective bosom and we'd all cry happy tears and that would have been that. Since it wasn't that way and I did write this book, I suppose the next person I really should thank is my father. Thank you, Alex Cumming, for siring me and ensuring I will always have lots of source material. I forgive you.

Thank you more, though, to Tommy Darling, for your patience, for waiting so many years for us to find you and for your story to be told. I wish I'd known you.

I hope I have demonstrated how much I appreciate and adore my mother, Mary Darling and my brother Tom with every fibre of my being. And if, as I suspect, Grant Shaffer actually is an alien from the planet Kindness, I will not be surprised. I will willingly give up these earthly delights and accompany him back there on the Mothership.

To all my dear friends who listened to this story or to me telling it to others over the many months, nay years, that it has taken for me to finally feel I am done with it: thank you.

Finally, the scariest thing about abuse of any shape or form, is, in my opinion, not the abuse itself, but that if it continues it can begin to feel commonplace and eventually acceptable. Writing this book and knowing it will be discussed around the world is in some way insurance for me that my story will never be thought of as commonplace, never acceptable, and for that I thank my publishers and everyone involved with making it happen from the bottom of my heart.

ALAN CUMMING
NYC, 2014

Alan Cumming is an award-winning actor, singer, writer, producer, and director. He starred in an acclaimed one-man staging of *Macbeth* on Broadway, and plays Eli Gold on the Emmy Award-winning television show *The Good Wife*. He won a Tony Award for his portrayal of the Emcee in the Broadway musical *Cabaret,* a role he reprised in a new staging in 2014. He has appeared in numerous films, including *The Anniversary Party, Spy Kids, X2:X Men United, Titus, Eyes Wide Shut,* and *Any Day Now.* He lives in New York and Edinburgh.